Diabetic Cookbook

for Beginners

1500-Days Simple and Easy Recipes to Manage Prediabetes and Type 2 Diabetes | Easy to Find Ingredients & No-stress Meal Plan

By

Kelly Smith

TABLE OF CONTENTS

INTRODUCTION

The Diabetic Cookbook is a comprehensive guide designed to help diabetic people manage their condition through a healthy and balanced diet. This cookbook features a collection of delicious and nutritious recipes tailored to meet the unique needs of people with diabetes. With a focus on delicious fresh fruits, vegetables, and other healthy ingredients, these recipes are designed to help regulate blood sugar levels, improve overall health, and provide essential vitamins and minerals. Whether you're new to juicing or are looking for new recipes to add to your routine, the Diabetic Cookbook has everything you need to start enjoying the many benefits of juicing for diabetes management.

The Diabetic Cookbook is a comprehensive guide for those looking to improve their nutrition, lose weight, and manage their diabetes through a proper diet. It offers a unique approach to managing diabetes by incorporating fresh, nutrient-rich recipes into one's diet. The recipes included in the book are carefully crafted to meet the unique needs of people with diabetes, taking into consideration factors such as calorie count, carbohydrate content, and the glycemic index of ingredients.

The book covers all aspects of delicious recipes for diabetes management, from the basics of a healthy and balanced diet and the benefits of incorporating such things into your diet to a comprehensive list of ingredients, tips on selecting and storing produce, and recipes for all occasions. The delicious recipes in the book are designed to be easy to prepare, delicious, and nutritious, providing a convenient and tasty way to get the nutrients and fiber your body needs.

In addition to recipes, the book also includes helpful information and tips on managing diabetes, such as the importance of monitoring blood sugar levels, ways to reduce the risk of complications, and practical advice on meal planning. Whether you're new to a balanced diet or are looking for new and healthy ways to manage your diabetes, the Diabetic Cookbook has everything you need to get started.

With its focus on a healthy and balanced diet, the Diabetic Cookbook is an essential resource for anyone looking to improve their health, manage their diabetes, and achieve their weight loss goals.

CHAPTER 1: WHAT IS DIABETES?

Diabetes is characterized by abnormally high amounts of blood glucose or blood sugar in the blood. The glucose in your bloodstream comes from the food you consume. Glucose is an essential source of fuel for the cells in your body. Insulin is a hormone that makes it easier for glucose to enter the body's cells. Insulin is responsible for this.

The inability of the body to manufacture insulin is one of the defining characteristics of type 1 diabetes. When you have diabetes, your body cannot create enough insulin or make good use of the insulin it produces. If you do not have an adequate amount of insulin in your body, glucose will build up in your blood, ultimately resulting in diabetes.

Foods that affect blood sugar levels

Certain foods, known as carbohydrates or "carbs," are the source of the sugar in your blood. Candies and other sweets, soft drinks, bread, tortillas, and white rice contain a high carbohydrate concentration. Your blood sugar level will rise directly to the number of carbohydrates you consume.

If you have diabetes of either type 1 or type 2, making smart decisions about the foods you eat is essential to maintaining appropriate blood sugar levels. If you can keep your blood sugar under control, you will minimize your risk of developing major health complications due to diabetes, such as loss of vision and issues with your heart.

Eating meals that maintain your blood sugar levels healthily will help prevent diabetes in the future, which is especially important if you have a history of diabetes or are at risk for having diabetes.

Diabetes is a serious health issue that affects millions of people in the United States. As of 2021, it is estimated that over 34 million people in the country have been diagnosed with diabetes, which is nearly 10% of the total population. It is estimated that another 88 million people have pre-diabetes, which indicates a high risk of developing diabetes near future. This number continues to rise each year.

The ever-increasing incidence of diabetes in the United States demonstrates how critical it is to find effective treatments for this ailment. Diabetes is a chronic condition that badly affects how the body processes glucose (sugar). It is a leading cause of serious health complications, such as heart disease, stroke, renal disease, and blindness. The condition can also lead to amputations. It can be a substantial struggle for people with diabetes to maintain control of their blood sugar levels through appropriate eating, regular physical exercise, and careful administration of their medication.

The rising percentage of diabetes in the United States puts a strain on the country's healthcare infrastructure, with direct and indirect costs estimated to amount to hundreds of billions of dollars each year. This highlights the need for ongoing research and advances in diabetes care, as well as the importance of diabetes prevention and management efforts, including education and awareness, lifestyle changes, and access to care.

Overall, the growing number of people with diabetes in the United States highlights the need for increased focus and resources on diabetes prevention and management, as well as the ongoing impact of this condition on public health and the healthcare system.

Diet for diabetes

There must be some specific diets or meal plans adaptable to each individual's needs. Your primary care physician may recommend that you consult with a registered dietician so that they can assist you in developing the optimal diet for you. The following will be taken into consideration by the plan:

Any medications that you now use; how much you weigh; any additional medical issues that you suffer from; your way of life and your preferences; your aspirations; eating the appropriate meals, in the appropriate amounts, at the appropriate times, and at the appropriate interval is a component shared by all diabetes diet programs.

Foods I can eat

Consuming a wide variety of nutritious foods from each of the following food groups is essential for managing diabetes effectively through diet:

Fruits and fresh vegetables

Whole grains, including wheat, brown rice, barley, oats, and quinoa, are healthier than refined grains.

Proteins, such as meat, chicken, turkeys, fish, eggs, nuts, fresh beans, lentils, and tofu

Proteins, such as meat, chicken, fresh turkey, fish, and eggs

Dairy products like milk, yogurt, and cheese are nonfat or low-fat.

Foods to avoid

You should consume fewer foods and beverages that are heavy in carbohydrates to maintain a healthy blood sugar level. This does not preclude the possibility that you will ever appreciate them. However, you will need to consume them less frequently or in lower quantities than usual.

Below are some foods to avoid:

Candies, delicious cookies, cake, ice cream, cereals, and canned fruits with sugar are foods high in sugar.

Juice, ordinary soda or soft drinks, and regular sports drinks are examples of beverages with added sugars.

White Rice, tortillas, bread, and pasta should be avoided.

Vegetables are high in starch, including white potatoes, corn, and peas.

You should reduce the amount of alcohol you consume and the amount of fat and salt in your diet.

Things to consider

If you have diabetes, you must consume the appropriate meals daily. Your eating plan will specify how much food you should consume at each meal and snack to consume the appropriate amount of carbohydrates. You will learn how to measure your food and count the carbohydrates in your food.

Consuming approximately the same number of carbohydrates at each meal can be beneficial.

You will also learn how to adhere to your eating

plan when you are eating at home as well as when you are eating in a restaurant.

Eating healthily to maintain control of your blood sugar levels requires some work. However, the reward is enjoying your life to the fullest while managing diabetes.

CHAPTER 3: BEST VEGETABLES AND FRUITS

For people with diabetes, choosing fruits and vegetables that are really low on the glycemic index and provide a steady source of nutrients and fiber is important. Some of the best options include:

Leafy greens: Spinach, kale, and lettuce are all low on GI and high in fiber and nutrients like vitamins A and C, iron, and calcium.

Berries: Berries such as strawberries, raspberries, and blueberries are low on the GI and high in fiber and antioxidants like anthocyanins and Vitamin C.

Cruciferous vegetables: Vegetables like broccoli, cauliflower, and Brussels sprouts are low in GI and high in fiber, vitamins, and minerals. They are also a great source of specific antioxidants.

Tomatoes are low on the GI and rich in fiber, vitamin C, and potassium.

Citrus fruits: Oranges, lemons, and limes are high in fiber and Vitamin C.

Avocado: Avocados have less healthy monounsaturated fats and antioxidants.

Apples: Apples are low on GI and high in fiber and antioxidants.

Incorporating these fruits and vegetables into your juicing regimen can help regulate blood sugar levels, improve nutrient intake, and support overall health and wellness.

CHAPTER 4: DIABETIC RECIPES FOR BREAKFAST

BAKED SMITH APPLES

Composition time: 0 minutes

Complete time: 5 minutes

Servings: 4

Components used:

- 4 Smith apples
- 21g chopped walnuts
- 28.3g raisins
- 2.84g cinnamon powder
- 1.42g honeydew powder
- 15g honey
- 15g unsalted butter, cut into small pieces
- 43g water

Method to cook:

1. Warm the cook stove to 375°F (190°C).
2. Slice the green apples and take off the cores using a sharp knife.
3. In a pot, mix the walnuts, raisins, cinnamon, and honeydew.
4. Stuff the apple cavities with the nut batter, dividing it evenly among the four apples.
5. Sprinkle each apple with honey and dot it with fresh butter.
6. Put the green apples in an oven tray and sprinkle water into the bottom of the tray.
7. Wrap the oven tray with a tin sheet and prepare for 30 minutes.
8. Take off the sheet and continue baking for extra 20-25 minutes or till the green apples are very soft when checked with a fork.
9. Serve warm, with any remaining juices spooned over the top.

Nutrients facts: Calories: 183 Fatty acids: 8.5 g Soaked Fatty acids: 2.5 g Lipids level: 10 mg Salt: 9 mg Total Starch level: 30 g Whole Fibre: 5 g Glucose: 22 g Amino acid level: 2 g

SPICED CONGEE WITH DATES

Composition time: 0 minutes

Complete time: 5 minutes

Servings: 4

Components used:

- 85 g long-grain white rice
- 64 oz water
- 4 dried dates, pitted and chopped
- 1 cinnamon
- 3 whole cloves
- 1.42g honeydew powder
- 1.42g ginger powder
- 1.42g salt
- 28.3g chopped almonds for garnish

Method to cook:

1. Soak the rice in fresh water till it runs clear.
2. In a large pot, add the rice, water, dates, cinnamon, cloves, honeydew, ginger, and some salt.
3. Boil the over moderate flame.
4. Reduce the flame and stew, mixing continuously, for 1-1 1/2 hours or till the rice has broken down and the brew has thickened to a porridge-like thickness.
5. Take off the cinnamon and cloves.
6. Divide the congee among serving dishes and sprinkle with chopped almonds.

Nutrients facts: Calories: 250 Fatty acids: 2 g Soaked Fatty acids: 0 g Lipids level: 0 mg Salt: 150 mg Total Starch level: 55 g Whole Fibre: 2 g Glucose: 5 g Amino acid level: 4 g

HAM AND CHEDDAR OMELETS

Composition time: 2 minutes

Complete time: 20 minutes

Servings: 2

Components used:

- 4 eggs
- 21g diced cooked ham
- 21g shredded cheddar cheese
- 28.3g chives

Salt

1. 15g unsalted butter
2. Method to cook:
3. Put the eggs into a pot and whisk till well beaten.
4. Sprinkle diced ham, shredded cheddar cheese chives, and some salt.
5. Soften the butter in a pan over moderate flame.

6. Include the egg batter to the tray and prepare for 2-3 minutes or till the bottom of the omelet is set.
7. Use a wooden stick to gently lift the corners of the omelet to cook well.
8. When the omelet is mostly set but still slightly runny on top, fold it in half with the wooden stick.
9. Cook for extra 1-2 minutes or till the omelet is cooked through.
10. Use the wooden stick to slide the omelet onto a serving plate.

Nutrients facts: Calories: 303 Fatty acids: 23 g Soaked Fatty acids: 11 g Lipids level: 425 mg Salt: 448 mg Total Starch level: 2 g Whole Fibre: 0 g Glucose: 1 g Amino acid level: 22 g

BASIC OATMEAL

Composition time: 0 minutes

Complete time: 10 minutes

Servings: 1

Components used:

- 43g rolled oats
- 85g water or milk
- Pinch of salt
- Optional seasonings: honey, maple extract, fruit, nuts, seeds, cinnamon

Method to cook:

1. In a cast iron pan, combine oats, water or milk, and some salt.
2. Boil the butter over a moderate flame, mixing continuously.
3. Reduce the flame and finely cook till oats are cooked to your desired thickness, mixing continuously.
4. Serve hot with your choice of seasonings.

Nutrients facts: Calories: 150 Fatty acids: 2.5 g Soaked Fatty acids: 0.5 g Lipids level: 0 mg Salt: 150 mg Total Starch level: 27 g Whole Fibre: 4 g Glucose: 0 g Amino acid level: 6 g

CHORIZO, TOMATO & GRILL CHILI FRITTATA

Composition time: 0 minutes

Complete time: 15 minutes

Servings: 4

Components used:

- 6 eggs
- 21g milk
- 1.42g salt
- 1.42g ground pepper
- 28.3g olive oil
- 43g diced chorizo sausage
- 43g diced tomato
- 21g diced grilled chili
- 21g cilantro

Method to cook:

1. Warm the cook stove to 176°C.
2. In a pot, mix and mix the eggs, milk, and some salt.
3. In a cook stove-safe frying pan, flames the olive oil over moderate flame.
4. Include the chorizo and prepare till browned, about 5 minutes.
5. Include the fresh tomato and grilled chili and prepare for extra 2-3 minutes.
6. Sprinkle egg batter over the chorizo batter in the tray.
7. Sprinkle with chopped cilantro.
8. Move the tray to the cook stove and prepare for 15-20 minutes or till the frittata is set in the center.
9. Take off from the cook stove and let chill for some time before cutting and serving.

Nutrients facts: Calories: 250 Fatty acids: 20 g Soaked Fatty acids: 6 g Lipids level: 240 mg Salt: 500 mg Total Starch level: 3 g Whole Fibre: 1 g Glucose: 1 g Amino acid level: 15 g

MUESLI WITH COCONUT, OATS & BANANAS

Composition time: 10 minutes

Complete time: 10 minutes

Servings: 2

Components used:

- 85g rolled oats
- 21g shredded coconut
- 21g chopped nuts (such as almonds or walnuts)
- 15g chia seeds
- 2.84g cinnamon powder
- 1.42g salt
- 15g honey
- 15g coconut oil
- 1 ripe banana, mashed
- 85g milk or yogurt

Method to cook:

1. In a pot, add the rolled oats, shredded coconut nuts, chia seeds, cinnamon powder, and some salt.
2. In a cast iron pan, soften the honey and coconut oil over a low flame, mixing continuously.
3. Include the mashed banana in the cast iron pan and stir till combined.
4. Sprinkle banana batter over the dry items and stir till oats and nuts are evenly coated.
5. Divide the muesli between two dishes.
6. Pour milk or yogurt over the muesli and shake to mix.
7. Allow the muesli to rest for some time to allow oats to absorb the liquid before eating.

Nutrients facts: Calories: 400 Fatty acids: 19 g Soaked Fatty acids: 10 g Lipids level: 0 mg Salt: 260 mg Total Starch level: 53 g Whole Fibre: 10 g Glucose: 23 g Amino acid level: 11 g

STEEL-CUT OATS

Composition time: 0 minutes

Complete time: 15 minutes

Servings: 4

Components used:

- 85g steel-cut oats
- 32oz water or milk
- 1.42g salt
- Optional seasonings: fresh fruit nuts, honey, cinnamon

Method to cook:

1. Soak the steel-cut oats in a porous basket and drain.
2. In a medium cast iron pan, bring the freshwater or milk to a seethe over moderate flame.
3. Include the steel-cut oats and some salt in the cast iron pan, and shake to mix.
4. Reduce the flame and stew oats, uncovered, for 20-30 minutes, mixing continuously, till oats are very soft.
5. Take off the cast iron pan from the flame and let the oats rest for some time before eating.
6. Divide oats into four dishes and garnish with desired seasonings, such as fresh fruit nuts, honey, or cinnamon.

Nutrients facts: Calories: 150 Fatty acids: 2 g Soaked Fatty acids: 0 g Lipids level: 0 mg Salt: 150 mg Total Starch level: 27 g Whole Fibre: 4 g Glucose: 0 g Amino acid level: 5 g

CRUMBLES WITH BERRIES, WALNUTS & OATS

Composition time: 0 minutes

Complete time: 25 minutes

Servings: 6

Components used: For the crumble:

- 85g rolled oats
- 43g flour
- 43g chopped walnuts
- 43g brown sugar
- 2.84g cinnamon powder
- 1.42g salt
- 85g unsalted butter

For the filling:

- 32oz berries
- 21g granulated sugar
- 15g cornstarch

Method to cook:

1. Warm the cook stove to 176°C.
2. In a pot, add the rolled oats, flour walnuts, brown sugar, cinnamon powder, and some salt.
3. Include the softened butter in the dry items and stir till the brew is crumbly.
4. In a different dish, toss the mixed berries with granulated sugar and cornstarch.
5. Divide the berry batter into six 6-ounce ramekins or an oven tray.
6. Top the berries with the crumble batter, dividing evenly.
7. Bake the crumbles for 25-30 minutes till the surface is cooked and the berries are bubbling.
8. Take off the crumbles from the cook stove and allow them to chill for some time before eating.

Nutrients facts: Calories: 450 Fatty acids: 23 g Soaked Fatty acids: 9 g Lipids level: 35 mg Salt: 105 mg Total Starch level: 61 g Whole Fibre: 7 g Glucose: 38 g Amino acid level: 5 g

BREAKFAST PANCAKES

Composition time: 10 minutes

Complete time: 10 minutes

Servings: 4

Components used:

- 1 43gs flour
- 2.84g baking powder
- 4.2g salt
- 15g granulated sugar
- 21g milk
- 1 egg
- 37g unsalted butter
- 4.2g vanilla extract
- Spray oil or additional butter for oiling the tray
- Optional seasonings: fresh fruit, maple extract, whipped cream

Method to cook:

1. In a pot, mix and mix all-purpose flour, baking powder, salt, and granulated sugar.
2. In a different dish, mix and mix the milk, egg butter, and vanilla extract.
3. Sprinkle wet items into the dry items and stir till mixed well.
4. Flame a frying pan or griddle over moderate flame.
5. Spray the tray or griddle with spray oil or lightly oil with additional butter.
6. Use a scoop to pour the brew onto the tray.
7. Cook the pancakes till golden brown on both sides.
8. Repeat with the leftover batter.
9. Serve the pancakes warm with desired seasonings, such as fresh fruit, maple extract, or whipped cream.

Nutrients facts: Calories: 340 Fatty acids: 11 g Soaked Fatty acids: 6 g Lipids level: 75 mg Salt: 830 mg Total Starch level: 50 g Whole Fibre: 1 g Glucose: 9 g Amino acid level: 9 g

MOCHA POTES WITH PEANUT BUTTER

Composition time: 0 minutes

Complete time: 5 minutes

Servings: 2

Components used:

- 43g rolled oats
- 1 21gs unsweetened almond milk
- 15g unsweetened cocoa powder
- 15g instant coffee powder
- 28.3g pure maple extract
- 21g smooth peanut butter

- Optional seasonings: sliced banana peanuts, chocolate chips

Method to cook:

1. In a medium cast iron pan, add the rolled oats, almond milk, cocoa powder, instant coffee powder, and maple extract.
2. Boil the butter over a moderate flame, mixing continuously to prevent sticking.
3. Cook the brew for 5-7 minutes, or till oats are very soft and the brew has thickened.
4. Divide the oatmeal batter between the two dishes.
5. Spoon some peanut butter on top of each dish.
6. Optional: Top with sliced banana peanuts, or chocolate chips.
7. Serve the mocha pots warm.

Nutrients facts: Calories: 350 Fatty acids: 18 g Soaked Fatty acids: 3 g Lipids level: 0 mg Salt: 220 mg Total Starch level: 42 g Whole Fibre: 7 g Glucose: 17 g Amino acid level: 10 g

GRANOLA BARS WITH CHERRY AND PECANS

Composition time: 0 minutes

Complete time: 30 minutes

Servings: 12 bars

Components used:

- 400g old-fashioned rolled oats
- 43g chopped pecans
- 43g dried cherries
- 21g honey
- 21g almond butter
- 21g coconut oil
- 4.2g vanilla extract
- 1.42g salt

Method to cook:

1. Warm the cook stove to 176°C. Line an 8x8 inch oven tray with baking paper.
2. In a pot, combine oats pecans, and dried cherries.
3. In a separate cast iron pan, add the honey, butter, coconut oil, vanilla extract, and some salt. Flame the brew over a moderate flame, mixing frequently, till the ingredients are softened and well mixed.
4. Sprinkle softened batter over the dry items and stir till everything is evenly coated.
5. Move the brew to the oven tray and use a wooden stick to press it firmly into the tray.

6. Bake till they are golden brown and fragrant.
7. Take off the tray from the cook stove and let it chill completely on a rack.
8. Once chilled, take off the granola bars from the tray by lifting the corners of the paper. Slice the bars into 12 even pieces.
9. Store the granola bars in a container for 7 days.

Nutrients facts: Calories: 220 Fatty acids: 12 g Soaked Fatty acids: 4 g Lipids level: 0 mg Salt: 50 mg Total Starch level: 26 g Whole Fibre: 3 g Glucose: 14 g Amino acid level: 4 g

PUMPKIN PUDDING WITH PEANUTS

Composition time: 10 minutes

Complete time: 60 minutes

Servings: 4

Components used:

- 15 oz pumpkin sauce
- 85g unsweetened almond milk
- 21g pure maple extract
- 4.2g cinnamon powder
- 2.84g ginger powder
- 1.42g honeydew powder
- 1.42g salt
- 21g chopped peanuts

Method to cook:

1. In a medium cast iron pan, add the pumpkin sauce, milk, maple extract, cinnamon powder, ginger, honeydew powder, and some salt.
2. Flame the brew over a moderate flame, mixing continuously, till it comes to a seethe.
3. Reduce the flame and cook the brew for 5-7 minutes, or till it has thickened and the flavors have melded together.
4. Divide the pumpkin pudding between four dishes or cups.
5. Sprinkle the chopped peanuts on top of each dish.
6. Serve the pumpkin pudding warm or chilled.

Nutrients facts: Calories: 160 Fatty acids: 7 g Soaked Fatty acids: 1 g Lipids level: 0 mg Salt: 200 mg Total Starch level: 24 g Whole Fibre: 5 g Glucose: 14 g Amino acid level: 4 g

GRANOLA BARS WITH ALMONDS AND BANANAS

Composition time: 10 minutes

Complete time: 25 minutes

Servings: 12 bars

Components used:

- 400g old-fashioned rolled oats
- 43g chopped almonds
- 43g mashed ripe banana (about 1 medium banana)
- 21g honey
- 21g almond butter
- 21g coconut oil
- 4.2g vanilla extract
- 1.42g salt

Method to cook:

1. Warm the cook stove to 176°C. Line an 8x8 inch oven tray with baking paper.
2. In a pot, combine oats and chopped almonds.
3. In a cast iron pan, add the banana, honey, almond butter, coconut oil, vanilla extract, and some salt. Flame the brew over a moderate flame, mixing frequently, till the ingredients are softened and well mixed.
4. Sprinkle softened batter over the dry items and stir till everything is evenly coated.
5. Move the brew to the oven tray and use a wooden stick to press it firmly and evenly into the tray.
6. Bake the granola bars till they are golden brown and fragrant.
7. Take off the tray from the cook stove and let it chill completely on a rack.
8. Once chilled, take off the granola bars from the tray by lifting the corners of the paper. Slice the bars into 12 even pieces.
9. Store the granola bars for up to a week.

Nutrients facts: Calories: 200 Fatty acids: 10 g Soaked Fatty acids: 4 g Lipids level: 0 mg Salt: 50 mg Total Starch level: 25 g Whole Fibre: 3 g Glucose: 12 g Amino acid level: 4 g

FROZEN BANANA GRAHAMS

Composition time: 10 minutes

Complete time: 2 hours

Servings: 4

Components used:

- 2 ripe bananas

- 43g low-fat vanilla Greek yogurt
- 4 whole graham crackers, broken into squares
- 21g mini chocolate chips (optional)

Method to cook:

1. Peel off the ripe bananas and chop them into small pieces. Put the small pieces in a layer on a baking sheet lined with baking paper. Freeze the banana in small pieces for up to 2 hours, or till frozen solid.
2. Once the small banana pieces are frozen, include them in a food processor along with the Greek yogurt. Pulse the brew till smooth and creamy.
3. Spread a spoonful of the banana batter onto each graham cracker square. If using, sprinkle mini chocolate chips on the banana batter.
4. Put the graham crackers on a baking sheet lined with baking paper and freeze for up to 1 hour, or till the banana batter is frozen and firm.
5. Serve the frozen banana grahams quickly, or store them in an airtight container in the freezer for up to 1 week.

Nutrients facts: Calories: 160 Fatty acids: 4.5 g Soaked Fatty acids: 2 g Lipids level: 3 mg Salt: 85 mg Total Starch level: 30 g Whole Fibre: 2 g Glucose: 15 g Amino acid level: 4 g

MEXICAN FRYING PAN-EGG CASSEROLE

Composition time: 5 minutes

Complete time: 10 minutes

Servings: 6

Components used:

- 15g olive oil
- 1 medium onion
- 1 bell pepper
- 4.2g cumin powder
- 4.2g smoked paprika
- 2.84g chili powder
- 1 can of black beans
- 1 can dice tomatoes
- 43g frozen corn kernels
- 6 eggs
- 21g cilantro

Method to cook:

1. Warm the cook stove to 375°F.
2. Flame the olive oil in a pan over moderate flame. Include the onion, red bell pepper,

and jalapeño pepper, and cook till the vegetables are soft.
3. Include the cumin, smoked paprika, and chili powder in the tray, and shake to mix.
4. Include the black beans, diced tomatoes, and frozen corn in the tray, and stir well.
5. Add the eggs to the vegetable batter, making sure to space them out evenly.
6. Put the tray in the Warmed cook stove and prepare for 10-12 minutes, or till the eggs are cooked to your liking.
7. Take off the tray from the cook stove and sprinkle the chopped cilantro on the casserole.
8. Season with salt and serve hot.

Nutrients facts: Calories: 201 Fatty acids: 8 g Soaked Fatty acids: 2 g Lipids level: 186 mg Salt: 325 mg Total Starch level: 22 g Whole Fibre: 7 g Glucose: 7 g Amino acid level: 13 g

ALMOND YOGHURT

Composition time: 0 minutes

Complete time: 5 minutes

Servings: 4

Components used:

- 85g raw almonds
- 32oz filtered water
- 28.3g maple extract
- 4.2g vanilla extract
- 15g lemon juice
- Pinch of sea salt

Method to cook:

1. Dip the almonds in water for up to 8 hours.
2. Drain and soak the almonds, then include them in a juicer or mixer with the filtered water. Mix till smooth and creamy.
3. Sprinkle almond batter through a nut milk bag or cheesecloth into a pot or jar, squeezing out as much liquid as possible.
4. Include the maple extract, vanilla essence, lemon juice, and salt in the pot or jar, and whisk to mix.
5. Wrap the pot or jar with a clean towel and let it rest for 6-12 hours, or till the brew thickens and develops a tangy flavor.
6. Once the brew has thickened, stir it well and move it to a container. Store for up to 5 days.

Nutrients facts (43g): Calories: 135 Fatty acids: 10 g Soaked Fatty acids: 1 g Lipids level: 0 mg Salt: 147

mg Total Starch level: 8 g Whole Fibre: 3 g Glucose: 4 g Amino acid level: 5 g

EGG CONFECTION

Composition time: 10 minutes

Complete time: 20 minutes

Difficulty Level: Easy

Serving: 2

Components used:

- a third cup of coconut oil
- 6 cardamom pods, crushed
- a quarter cup of almond powder
- 28g powdered milk
- 21g stevia 8 eggs
- 8.4g chopped almonds

Method to cook:

- Warm the coconut oil in the Instant Pot's cook mode.
- Cook, mixing constantly, till the cardamom pods and almond powder is fragrant (approximately 5 minutes.)
- Sprinkle dry milk powder and boil till golden brown (approximately 6 minutes.)
- In a pot, mix and mix the eggs and stevia till smooth.
- Sprinkle egg batter into the Instant Pot and give it a good swirl.
- Continue to cook till the oil separates from the milk.
- Move to serve dishes from the Instant Pot.
- Sprinkle chopped almonds on top.
- Put the food on the table.

Nutrients facts: 277 calories, 13 g fatty acid, 16 g starch, 24 g Amino acid

Glycemic Index: Low

BOSTON BROWN BREAD

Composition time: 10 minutes

Complete time: 40 minutes

Difficulty Level: Easy

Servings: 8-10

Components used:

- 85g cornmeal
- 85g rye flour
- 85g whole flour

- 4.2g baking soda
- 4.2g salt
- 85g buttermilk
- 85g molasses
- 85g raisins
- Butter or spray oil for greasing

Method to cook:

1. Warm the cook stove to 325°F (165°C). Oil a 2-quart (2-liter) cook a stove-safe dish or a 9x5 inch (23x13 cm) loaf pan with fresh butter or oil spray.
2. In a pot, mix and mix the cornmeal, rye flour, whole flour, baking soda, and some salt till well mixed.
3. Include the buttermilk and molasses in the dry items and stir till well mixed.
4. Fold in the raisins.
5. Sprinkle batter into the oiled dish or loaf pan and smooth out the top.
6. Wrap the pot or pan with a sheet and place it into a large oven tray.
7. Bake for 2 to 2 hours.
8. Take off the bread from the cook stove and let it chill for up to 10 minutes before removing it from the pot or pan.
9. Slice the bread and serve it warm.

Nutrients facts: Calories: 342 Fatty acids: 2 g Soaked Fatty acids: 1 g Lipids level: 3 mg Salt: 589 mg Total Starch level: 77 g Whole Fibre: 6 g Glucose: 40 g Amino acid level: 7 g

BREAKFAST COOKIES

Composition time: 5 minutes

Complete time: 40 minutes

Servings: 12 cookies

Components used:

- 1 43gs rolled oats
- 43g almond powder
- 43g unsweetened shredded coconut
- 43g dried cranberries
- 43g chopped nuts (such as almonds, pecans, or walnuts)
- 21g honey
- 21g softened coconut oil
- 1 egg
- 4.2g vanilla extract
- 2.84g cinnamon
- 1.42g salt

Method to cook:

1. Warm the cook stove to 176°C.

2. In a pot, add the rolled oats, almond powder, shredded coconut, dried cranberries, and chopped nuts.
3. In a different dish, mix and mix the honey coconut oil, egg, vanilla extract, cinnamon, and some salt till well mixed.
4. Sprinkle wet items into the dry items and stir till well mixed.
5. Make the cookies with the back of a spoon.
6. Bake till the cookies are cooked well.
7. Remove from the stove and allow them to chill on the baking sheet before moving them to a rack to chill completely.

Nutrients facts: Calories: 192 Fatty acids: 12 g Soaked Fatty acids: 5 g Lipids level: 16 mg Salt: 57 mg Total Starch level: 20 g Whole Fibre: 3 g Glucose: 10 g Amino acid level: 4 g

WAFFLES WITH CHEDDAR AND SAGE

Composition time: 10 minutes

Complete time: 15 minutes

Serving: 2

Components used:

- 85g almond powder
- 21g coconut powder
- 8.4g baking powder
- 1.42g salt
- 1.42g ground pepper
- 21g sage
- 6oz unsweetened almond milk
- 2 eggs
- 21g shredded cheddar cheese
- 15g olive oil

Method to cook:

1. Warm your waffle maker.
2. In a pot, mix and mix almond powder, coconut powder, baking powder, salt, and ground pepper. Pour chopped sage.
3. In a different dish, mix and mix almond milk, eggs, shredded cheddar cheese, and olive oil.
4. Sprinkle wet items into the dry items and stir till mixed well.
5. Spray your waffle maker with spray oil.
6. Sprinkle batter into the waffle maker and prepare according to the manufacturer's instructions.
7. Serve the waffles warm, topped with additional shredded cheddar cheese and chopped sage, if desired.

Nutrients facts

- Calories: 261
- Fatty acids: 21g
- Soaked Fatty acids: 5g
- Lipids level: 108mg
- Salt: 419mg
- Total Starch: 8g
- Whole Fibre: 4g
- Sugars: 1g
- Amino acid level: 12g

ITALIAN SCRAMBLE

Composition time: 10 minutes

Complete time: 10 minutes

Serving: 2

Components used:

- 2 eggs
- 21g tomatoes
- 21g spinach
- 21g onion
- 21g bell pepper
- 15g olive oil
- Salt
- 21g grated Parmesan cheese

Method to cook:

1. Flame the olive oil in a pan over moderate flame.
2. Include the diced onions and peppers and cook for 2-3 minutes, or till the onions are translucent.
3. Include the diced tomatoes and chopped spinach on the tray, and shake to mix with the onion and bell pepper batter.
4. In a different dish, beat the eggs together till well mixed.
5. Sprinkle beaten eggs into the tray with the vegetables and stir gently till the eggs are fully cooked about 2-3 minutes.
6. Season with Salt.
7. Sprinkle with grated Parmesan cheese and serve hot.

Nutrients facts:

- Total Servings: 2
- Size: 1/2 of the recipe
- Calories: 199
- Fatty acids: 14g
- Soaked Fatty acids: 4g
- Trans Fat: 0g
- Lipids level: 192mg
- Salt: 337mg

- Total Starch level: 6g
- Whole Fibre: 2g
- Sugars: 3g
- Amino acid level: 14g

CREAM CHEESE-FILLED PANCAKES

Composition time: 10 minutes

Complete time: 10 minutes

Servings: 4 pancakes

Components used:

- 85g flour
- 15g granulated sugar
- 4.2g baking powder
- 2.84g baking soda
- 1.42g salt
- 85g buttermilk
- 1 egg
- 28.3g unsalted butter
- 2.84g vanilla extract
- 4oz cheese
- 28.3g ground sugar
- 2.84g vanilla essence

Method to cook:

1. In a pot, mix and mix the dry items.
2. In a different dish, mix and mix the buttermilk, egg butter, and vanilla extract till well mixed.
3. Sprinkle wet items into the dry items and stir till mixed well (there should still be lumps in the brew).
4. In another dish, beat together the cheese, ground sugar, and vanilla extract till smooth.
5. Warm a nonstick griddle or frying pan over moderate flame.
6. Pour 21g of pancake batter onto the griddle for each pancake.
7. Quickly spoon about 28.3g of the cream cheese batter onto the center of each pancake.
8. Wrap the cream cheese filling with a small amount of pancake batter, about 15g. Cook the pancakes till bubbles form on the surface and the corners are dry about 2-3 minutes.
9. Use a wooden stick to flip the pancakes and prepare for 1-2 minutes on the other side till golden brown.
10. Repeat with the leftover batter and cream cheese batter.
11. Serve the pancakes warm with your favorite seasonings.

Nutrients facts: Calories: 297 Fatty acids: 15 g Soaked Fatty acids: 8 g Lipids level: 88 mg Salt: 486 mg Total Starch level: 31 g Whole Fibre: 1 g Glucose: 9 g Amino acid level: 8 g

CARAMEL BREAD PUDDING

Composition time: 10 minutes

Complete time: 40 minutes

Servings: 6-8

Components used:

- 8 slices white bread
- 400g milk + 3 eggs
- 43g granulated sugar
- 2.84g vanilla extract
- 1.42g cinnamon powder
- Pinch of salt
- 43g caramel sauce
- Whipped cream and additional caramel sauce for serving (optional)

Method to cook:

1. Warm the cook stove to 176°C. Oil a square oven tray.
2. Slice the bread into small pieces and put them in the oven tray.
3. In a pot, mix and mix the milk, eggs, sugar, vanilla extract, cinnamon and some salt till well mixed. Sprinkle egg batter over the bread pieces and press down with a spoon to make sure all of the bread is coated. Allow the brew to rest for 10-15 minutes to allow the bread to absorb the liquid.
4. Sprinkle the caramel sauce on the bread pudding.
5. Bake for 40-45 minutes, or till the pudding is set and the top is golden brown.
6. Allow the pudding to chill for some time before eating.

Nutrients facts: Calories: 251 Fatty acids: 7 g Soaked Fatty acids: 3 g Lipids level: 81 mg Salt: 291 mg Total Starch level: 42 g Whole Fibre: 0 g Glucose: 30 g Amino acid level: 6 g

EGGS WITH BASIL & TOMATO

Composition time: 10 minutes

Complete time: 10 minutes

Servings: 2

Components used:

- 4 eggs
- 15g olive oil
- 1 small tomato
- 28.3g basil
- Salt

Method to cook:

1. Warm the olive oil in a pan. Include the tomato pieces to the tray and cook for 2-3 minutes.
2. Add the eggs to the tray and season with Salt.
3. Cook the eggs to your desired level of doneness, mixing continuously and breaking up the yolks if desired.
4. Sprinkle the chopped basil over the eggs and continue preparing for another minute or till the eggs are fully cooked and the basil is slightly wilted.
5. Serve the eggs hot with toast or crusty bread.

Nutrients facts: Calories: 182 Fatty acids: 14 g Soaked Fatty acids: 3 g Lipids level: 372 mg Salt: 148 mg Total Starch level: 2 g Whole Fibre: 0 g Glucose: 1 g Amino acid level: 12 g

ACORN SQUASH WITH STUFFING

Composition time: 0 minutes

Complete time: 10 minutes

Serving: 2

Components used:

- 2 acorn squash, halved and seeded
- 28.3g butter
- 43g diced onion
- 43g diced celery
- 43g diced carrot
- 1 clove garlic, minced
- 2.84g dried thyme
- 2.84g dried sage
- 2.84g dried rosemary
- 400g cubed bread
- 21g parsley
- 21g chives
- 21g basil
- 43g vegetable broth
- Salt

Method to cook:

1. Warm cook stove to 375°F.
2. Put the acorn squash halves cut-side down in an oven tray and add about 1/2 inch of water to the bottom of the tray. Bake for about 30 minutes or till the squash is very soft.
3. While the squash is baking, soften the butter in a large frying pan over moderate flame. Include the onion, celery, and carrot, and prepare for about 5 minutes or till the vegetables are soft.
4. Include the garlic, thyme, sage, and rosemary to the tray and prepare for another 2 minutes.
5. Sprinkle bread pieces, parsley, chives, and basil. Include the vegetable broth and stir till the bread pieces are moistened.
6. Season with Salt.
7. Take off the squash halves from the cook stove and flip them over. Divide the stuffing batter between the four squash halves.
8. Return the squash to the cook stove and prepare for another 20-25 minutes or till the stuffing is golden brown and crispy.
9. Serve hot and enjoy!

Nutritional information (per serving): Calories: 235 Fat: 7g Starchs: 45g Fibre: 7g Amino acid level: 5g Salt: 560mg

MUSSELS STEAMED IN COCONUT BROTH

Composition time: 10 minutes

Complete time: 10 minutes

Serving: 2

Components used:

- 2 lbs mussels
- 15g olive oil
- 1 onion
- 2 cloves garlic, minced
- 4.2g grated fresh ginger
- 1 can (14 oz) coconut milk
- 15g red curry paste
- 15g fish sauce
- 15g lime juice
- 28.3g cilantro

Method to cook:

1. Scrub the mussels with a brush and soak them in cold water. Discard any mussels with broken shells or that do not close when tapped.

2. Flame the olive oil in a large pot over a moderate flame. Include the onion and prepare till softened, about 5 minutes.

3. Include the garlic and ginger and prepare for 1 minute.

4. Sprinkle coconut milk, red curry paste, and fish sauce. Bring to a seethe.

5. Include the mussels in the pot, cover, and prepare till the mussels have opened about 5-7 minutes. Discard any mussels that do not open.

6. Sprinkle lime juice and cilantro.

7. Divide the mussels and broth among dishes and serve hot.

Nutrients facts: This recipe serves 4 people and each serving contains approximately:

- Calories: 315
- Fatty acids: 19g
- Soaked Fatty acids: 13g
- Lipids level: 42mg
- Salt: 870mg
- Total Starch level: 13g
- Whole Fibre: 1g
- Sugar: 2g
- Amino acid level: 22g

CARAMELIZED ONIONS

Composition time: 10 minutes

Complete time: 10 minutes

Serving: 2

Components used:

- 2 large onions
- 28.3g olive oil
- 2.84g salt
- 2.84g sugar
- 15g balsamic vinegar (optional)

Method to cook:

1. Peel and slice the onions thinly.
2. In a large frying pan, flame the olive oil over moderate flame.
3. Include the sliced onions and shake to coat them with the oil.
4. Sprinkle the salt and sugar over the onions and shake to mix.
5. Cook the onions over medium-low flame, mixing continuously for 30 to 40 minutes or till they are soft and caramelized.
6. If desired, Sprinkle balsamic vinegar during the last few minutes of cooking.
7. Serve hot or.

Nutritional information (per serving):

Calories: 93, Fat: 7g, Starchs: 8g, Fibre: 1g, Amino acid level: 1g, Salt: 198mg

ITALIAN-STYLE STUFFED TOMATOES

Composition time: 10 minutes

Complete time: 10 minutes

Serving: 2

Components used:

- 4 medium tomatoes
- 43g cooked quinoa
- 21g chopped onion
- 21g chopped red bell pepper
- 21g chopped zucchini
- 21g chopped mushrooms
- 15g minced garlic
- 1.42g dried oregano
- 1.42g dried basil
- Salt and ground pepper, to taste
- 21g grated Parmesan cheese
- 15g olive oil

Method to cook:

1. Warm the cook stove to 375°F (190°C).
2. Cut off the tops of the fresh tomatoes and scoop out the insides, leaving a shell.
3. In a pot, mix the quinoa, onion, red bell pepper, zucchini, mushrooms, garlic, oregano, basil, salt, ground pepper, and Parmesan cheese.
4. Spoon the quinoa batter into the fresh tomato shells, pressing down to fill them completely.
5. Sprinkle the olive oil on each stuffed tomato.
6. Put the stuffed tomatoes in an oven tray and prepare for 30-35 minutes or till the fresh tomatoes are very soft and the stuffing is golden brown.
7. Take off from the cook stove and let chill for some time before eating.

Nutritional Information (per serving): Calories: 134 Fatty acids: 6.5g Soaked Fatty acids: 1.5g Lipids level: 4mg Salt: 135mg Total Starch level: 15g Whole Fibre: 3g Sugars: 5g Amino acid level: 6g

GREEK GREEN BEANS & TOMATOES

Composition time: 10 minutes

Complete time: 10 minutes

Serving: 2

Components used:

- 1 lb green beans, trimmed
- 28g olive oil
- 1 large onion
- 4 cloves garlic, minced
- 1 can (14.5 oz) diced tomatoes

- 15g dried oregano
- 1/28g salt
- 1/4 tsp ground pepper
- 21g parsley
- 21g crumbled feta cheese (optional)

Method to cook:

1. In a large frying pan, flame olive oil over moderate flame. Include the chopped onion and prepare till softened, about 5 minutes.
2. Include the minced garlic and prepare for another minute.
3. Include the green beans, diced tomatoes (with their juices), dried oregano, salt, and ground pepper in the tray. Stir everything together.
4. Reduce the flame, Wrap the tray, and allow the green beans to stew for about 20-25 minutes or till they are very soft.
5. Once the green beans are done, take off the tray from the flame and Sprinkle chopped parsley. Sprinkle crumbled feta cheese over the top if desired.

Nutrients facts: Makes about 4 servings

Per serving: 149 calories, 9.6g fatty acid, 14.4g starch, 4.4g Fibre, 4.2g Amino acid

ORANGE FLAVORED CARROTS

Composition time: 10 minutes

Complete time: 15 minutes

Serving: 2

Components used:

- 4 large carrots, peeled and sliced into thin rounds
- 28g butter
- 15g honey
- 15g orange juice
- 15g orange zest
- Some salt, to taste
- Fresh parsley (optional)

Method to cook:

1. Soften the butter in a frying pan over moderate flame.
2. Include the sliced carrots and cook for 5-6 minutes, mixing continuously, till they begin to soften.
3. Include the honey, orange juice, and orange zest in the tray, and shake to coat the carrots.

4. Continue preparing the carrots for another 3-4 minutes, till they are very soft and the liquid has thickened.
5. Season the carrots with Salt.
6. Move the carrots to a serving dish and sprinkle with fresh parsley, if desired.

Nutrients facts:

Calories: 90, Fat: 5g, Starchs: 12g, Fibre: 3g, Sugar: 8g, Amino acid level: 1g, Salt: 115mg

ROASTED BEANS, PARSNIPS & GARLIC

Composition time: 5 minutes

Complete time: 10 minutes

Serving: 2

Components used:

- 1 can of white beans, drained and soaked
- 2 parsnips, peeled and chopped into small pieces
- 6-8 cloves of garlic, peeled
- 15g of olive oil
- Salt

Method to cook:

1. Warm your cook stove to 375°F (190°C).
2. Put the drained and soaked white beans parsnips, and peeled garlic cloves in a pot.
3. Sprinkle with olive oil and sprinkle with some salt. Toss everything together to make sure the veggies and beans are well coated.
4. Move the brew to an oven tray or a baking sheet.
5. Roast in the Warmed cook stove for about 25-30 minutes or till the vegetables are very soft and slightly caramelized.
6. Serve as a side dish or add to a salad for extra Amino acid and Fibre.

Nutritional information (per serving): Calories: 200, Fatty acids: 4g, Soaked Fatty acids: 1g, Lipids level: 0mg, Salt: 450mg, Total Starch level: 35g, Whole Fibre: 9g, Sugars: 6g, Amino acid level: 10g

CHEDDAR WITH BLACK OLIVES

Composition time: 0 minutes

Complete time: 10 minutes

Serving: 2

Components used:

- 1 pound cheddar cheese, rated
- 43g black olives, pitted and chopped
- 28.3g parsley
- 1.42g garlic powder
- 1.42g onion powder
- Some salt, to taste

Method to cook:

1. In a pot, add the grated cheddar cheese black olives, parsley, garlic powder, and onion powder. Mix well.
2. Add Salt, and mix well again.
3. Move the brew to a serving dish and refrigerate for up to 1 hour before eating.

Nutritional information (per serving):

- Calories: 220
- Fat: 18g
- Starches: 2g
- Amino acid level: 13g
- Sugar: 0g
- Salt: 440mg

BULGUR ALMOND & COCONUT SIDE

Composition time: 10 minutes

Complete time: 10 minutes

Serving: 2

Components used:

- 85g bulgur
- 400g water
- 43g shredded unsweetened coconut
- 43g chopped almonds
- 21g olive oil
- 21g lemon juice
- Salt and ground pepper to taste

Method to cook:

1. Soak the bulgur under running water in a fine-mesh strainer and drain well.
2. In a large cast iron pan, bring 400g of water to a seethe.
3. Include the bulgur and Reduce the flame. Stew for 10-12 minutes or till the freshwater has been absorbed and the bulgur is very soft.
4. Meanwhile, Warm the cook stove to 176°C (180°C). Spread the shredded coconut and chopped almonds on a baking sheet and roast for 8-10 minutes or till golden brown.
5. In a pot, mix and mix the olive oil, lemon juice, salt, and ground pepper.
6. Include the cooked bulgur in the pot and toss well to coat with the dressing.
7. Include the roasted coconut and almonds in the pot and mix well.
8. Serve warm or.

Nutritional information (per serving):

- Calories: 248
- Fatty acids: 16.3g
- Soaked Fatty acids: 4.7g
- Lipids level: 0mg
- Salt: 87mg
- Total Starch level: 22.4g
- Whole Fibre: 6.4g
- Sugars: 1.7g
- Amino acid level: 5.7g

TURNIPS & MASHED POTATOES

Composition time: 5 minutes

Complete time: 5 minutes

Serving: 2

Components used:

- 2 large turnips, peeled and chopped
- 2 large potatoes, peeled and chopped
- 4 tbsp unsalted butter
- 21g milk
- Some salt, to taste

Method to cook:

1. In a large pot, bring water to a seethe. Include the chopped turnips and potatoes, and boil till very soft (about 20 minutes).
2. Drain the turnips and potatoes and return them to the pot.
3. Include butter, milk, and some salt. Mash the turnips and potatoes using a potato masher or a fork.
4. Stir everything together till the mashed turnips and potatoes are smooth and creamy.

5. Serve hot as a side dish.

Nutritional Information (per serving): Calories: 184 Fatty acids: 9g Soaked Fatty acids: 6g Lipids level: 24mg Salt: 49mg Total Starch: 24g Whole Fibre: 4g Glucose: 5g Amino acid level: 4g

SMOKEY DIPPING POTATO FRIES

Composition time: 10 minutes

Complete time: 10 minutes

Serving: 2

Components used:

- 4 large russet potatoes, cut into thin fries
- 15g olive oil
- 4.2g smoked paprika
- 2.84g garlic powder
- 2.84g onion powder
- 2.84g salt
- 1.42g ground pepper
- 43g mayonnaise
- 15g lemon juice
- 2.84g smoked paprika
- 1.42g garlic powder
- 1.42g onion powder
- 1.42g salt

Method to cook:

1. Warm cook stove to 400°F (200°C). Line a large baking sheet with baking paper.

2. In a pot, toss the potato fries with olive oil, smoked paprika, garlic powder, onion powder, salt, and ground pepper. Arrange the fries in a single layer on the baking sheet.

3. Bake for 20 to 25 minutes or till crispy and golden brown, flipping the fries halfway through cooking.

4. While the fries are baking, prepare the dipping sauce. In a pot, mix and mix the mayonnaise, lemon juice, smoked paprika, garlic powder, onion powder, and some salt till smooth.

5. Serve the hot fries with the dipping sauce on the side.

Nutrient facts: This recipe makes 4 servings. Each serving contains approximately:

Calories: 480, Fat: 29g, Starchs: 48g, Fibre: 4g, Sugar: 2g, Amino acid level: 5g

MASHED POTATOES WITH ROASTED GARLIC

Composition time: 10 minutes

Complete time: 10 minutes

Serving: 2

Components used:

- 2 pounds of potatoes, peeled and cut into small pieces
- 4 cloves garlic, peeled and left whole
- 43g milk
- 28.3g butter
- Salt
- parsley, for garnish

Method to cook:

1. Warm the cook stove to 400°F.
2. Put the potatoes and garlic in a large pot and cover with water. Bring to a seethe and then Reduce the flame to a seethe. Cook for 20-25 minutes or till the potatoes are very soft when checked with a fork.
3. While the potatoes are cooking, soften the butter in a cast iron pan over a low flame.
4. Drain the potatoes and garlic and return them to the pot.
5. Mash the potatoes and garlic together with a potato masher or fork.
6. Include the softened butter, milk, and some salt in the pot and stir till well mixed.
7. Continue to mash and stir the potatoes till they reach your desired thickness.
8. Move the mashed potatoes to a serving dish and sprinkle with chopped parsley. Serve hot.

Nutritional information (per serving):

Calories: 190, Starchs: 28g, Amino acid level: 4g, Fat: 7g, Soaked Fatty acids: 4g, Lipids level: 19mg, Salt: 77mg, Fibre: 3g, Sugar: 2g

RICE & BEAN FRYING PAN

Composition time: 10 minutes

Complete time: 10 minutes

Serving: 2

Components used:

- 85g brown rice
- 400g vegetable broth or water
- 15g olive oil
- 1 onion, diced
- 2 cloves garlic, minced

- 1 bell pepper, diced
- 1 zucchini, diced
- 1 can black beans, drained and soaked
- 15g chili powder
- 1/28g cumin
- Some salt, to taste
- 21g cilantro

Method to cook:

1. In a medium pot, combine brown rice and vegetable broth. Bring to a seethe, then Lowerflame to low and stew, covered, for about 45 minutes or till the rice is cooked.
2. Flame olive oil in a large frying pan over moderate flame. Add onion and garlic, and cook for 2-3 minutes till fragrant.
3. Add bell pepper and zucchini, and cook for 5-7 minutes till the vegetables are very soft.
4. Add black beans, chili powder, cumin, and some salt. Stir well and prepare for 2-3 minutes.
5. Add cooked brown rice to the tray and stir till combined.
6. Garnish with chopped cilantro and serve.

Nutrient facts: This recipe yields 4 servings. Each serving contains approximately:

Calories: 316, Fatty acids: 6g, Soaked Fatty acids: 1g, Trans fat: 0g, Lipids level: 0mg, Salt: 597mg, Total Starch level: 56g, Whole Fibre: 11g, Sugars: 4g, Amino acid level: 12g

TOMATOES IN STEWED SAUCE

Composition time: 0 minutes

Complete time: 10 minutes

Serving: 2

Components used:

- 4 large tomatoes
- 1 large onion
- 2 cloves garlic, minced
- 28.3g olive oil
- 4.2g paprika
- 4.2g ground cumin
- 4.2g ground coriander
- 2.84g cinnamon
- 2.84g salt
- 1.42g ground pepper
- 85g vegetable broth
- 28.3g tomato paste
- 28.3g parsley

Method to cook:

1. In a large frying pan, flame the olive oil over moderate flame. Include the chopped onion and minced garlic, and cook till the onion is translucent about 5 minutes.
2. Include the chopped tomatoes on the tray and shake to mix. Sprinkle the paprika, cumin, coriander, cinnamon, and some salt over the fresh tomatoes, and shake to coat the vegetables in the spices.
3. Sprinkle vegetable broth into the tray and include the fresh tomato paste. Stir well to mix and bring the brew to a seethe.
4. Reduce the flame and stew the fresh tomatoes in the stewed sauce for about 20-25 minutes, mixing continuously till the sauce has thickened and the vegetables are very soft.
5. Sprinkle chopped parsley just before eating.

Nutritional Information (per serving):

Calories: 110, Fatty acids: 7g, Soaked Fatty acids: 1g, Lipids level: 0mg, Salt: 435mg, Total Starch: 11g, Whole Fibre: 3g, Sugars: 6g, Amino acid level: 2g

ORANGE GLAZED CARROTS

Composition time: 0 minutes

Complete time: 50 minutes

Serving: 2

Components used:

- 1 pound carrots, peeled and sliced
- 21g orange juice
- 21g honey
- 28.3g butter
- Salt
- parsley, for garnish (optional)

Method to cook:

1. In a large frying pan, soften butter over moderate flame. Add sliced carrots and cook for about 5 minutes, mixing continuously, till they start to become very soft.
2. In a pot, mix and mix orange juice and honey till well mixed.
3. Pour orange juice and honey batter over the carrots and shake to coat evenly.
4. Lower the flame to low and Wrap the tray. Allow the carrots to cook for about 10

     minutes, mixing continuously till they are
     very soft and glazed with the orange sauce.

5.   Season with Salt.

6.   Move the carrots to a serving dish and
      garnish with parsley, if desired.

Nutrients facts:

Calories: 120, Fat: 3g, Starchs: 24g, Fibre: 3g,
Amino acid level: 1g, Salt: 90mg

SHRIMP FRIED RICE

Composition time: 0 minutes

Complete time: 10 minutes

Serving: 2

Components used:

- 400g of cooked rice
- 1/2 pound shrimp, peeled and deveined
- 43g frozen peas and carrots
- 21g chopped onion
- 2 cloves garlic, minced
- 2 eggs, lightly beaten
- 28.3g soy sauce
- 28.3g vegetable oil
- Salt

Method to cook:

1. Flame the vegetable oil in a large frying pan over moderate flame. Include the shrimp and prepare till pink, about 2-3 minutes. Take off from the frying pan and set aside.
2. Include the onion, garlic, frozen peas, and carrots in the tray. Cook for 2-3 minutes, mixing continuously.
3. Include the cooked rice in the tray and stir till well mixed with the vegetables.
4. Push the rice batter to the sides of the tray, creating a well in the center. Include the beaten eggs in the well and scramble till cooked through.
5. Return the cooked shrimp to the tray and Sprinkle soy sauce.
6. Season with Salt.
7. Serve hot.

Nutritional information (per serving): Calories: 315 Fatty acids: 11.9g Soaked Fatty acids: 2.4g Lipids level: 167mg Salt: 776mg Total Starch: 31.4g Whole Fibre: 1.9g Glucose: 1.6g Amino acid level: 19.2g

TUNA KEBABS

Composition time: 5 minutes

Complete time: 15 minutes

Serving: 2

Components used:

- 1 lb fresh tuna, cut into 1-inch cubes
- 28g olive oil
- 15g lemon juice
- 15g honey
- 15g soy sauce
- 1 garlic clove, minced
- Some salt, to taste
- Wooden skewers, soaked in water for 30 minutes

Method to cook:

1. Warm the grill to a moderate flame.
2. In a pot, mix and mix the olive oil, lemon juice, honey, soy sauce, minced garlic, and some salt.
3. Include the tuna cubes in the marinade and toss to coat well. Allow the tuna to marinate for 10-15 minutes.
4. Thread the tuna onto the soaked wooden skewers, leaving a little space between each piece.
5. Grill the tuna kebabs for 2-3 minutes per side or till cooked through and slightly charred.
6. Serve the tuna kebabs hot, garnished with herbs or a squeeze of lemon juice.

Nutritional information (per serving):

Calories: 275, Fat: 12g, Amino acid level: 34g, Starchs: 5g, Fibre: 0g, Sugar: 4g, Salt: 384mg

PARMESAN-CRUSTED TILAPIA WITH ALMONDS

Composition time: 10 minutes

Complete time: 50 minutes

Serving: 2

Components used:

- 4 tilapia fillets
- 43g almond powder
- 43g grated parmesan cheese

- 21g chopped almonds
- 21g olive oil
- 28.3g parsley
- Some salt, to taste

Method to cook:

1. Warm the cook stove to 375°F (190°C).
2. In a pot, mix the almond powder, parmesan cheese almonds, and some salt.
3. Brush each tilapia fillet with olive oil.
4. Coat each fillet with the almond powder batter, pressing the brew onto the fish.
5. Put the fillets on a baking sheet lined with baking paper and prepare for 12-15 minutes, or till the fish flakes easily with a fork and the crust is golden brown.
6. Sprinkle chopped parsley over the fish and serve.

Nutritional Information (per serving): Calories: 356 Fat: 23.7g Amino acid level: 31.1g Starchs: 3.8g Fibre: 1.8g Sugar: 0.8g Salt: 471mg

SALMON CROQUETTES

Composition time: 10 minutes

Complete time: 10 minutes

Serving: 2

Components used:

- 2 cans (14.75 oz each) salmon, drained
- 43g bread crumbs
- 21g chopped onion
- 21g chopped celery
- 21g chopped bell pepper
- 2 cloves garlic, minced, and 15g lemon juice
- 8.4g Dijon mustard
- 2.84g dried dill
- 2.84g salt
- 1.42g ground pepper
- 2 eggs, lightly beaten
- 28.3g olive oil

Method to cook:

1. In a pot, add the drained salmon, bread crumbs, onion, celery, bell pepper, garlic, lemon juice, Dijon mustard, dill, salt, and ground pepper. Mix well.
2. Include the beaten eggs in the brew and stir till everything is evenly combined.
3. Form the brew into small patties, about 2-3 inches in diameter.

4. Flame the olive oil in a large frying pan over moderate flame.
5. Once the oil is hot, include the salmon patties on the tray, making sure they do not touch each other.
6. Cook the salmon patties for about 3-4 minutes on each side till they are golden brown and prepared through.
7. Serve hot with your choice of side dish.

Nutritional information (per serving):

Calories: 254, Fatty acids: 14g, Soaked Fatty acids: 2g, Lipids level: 116mg, Salt: 625mg, Total Starch: 7g, Whole Fibre: 1g, Sugars: 1g, Amino acid level: 23g

THAI PEANUT SHRIMP CURRY

Composition time: 10 minutes

Complete time: 15 minutes

Serving: 2

Components used:

- 1 lb large shrimp, peeled and deveined
- 1 red bell pepper, thinly sliced
- 1 yellow bell pepper, thinly sliced
- 1 small onion, diced
- 2 cloves garlic, minced
- 15g ginger, minced
- 1 can coconut milk
- 21g creamy peanut butter
- 28g red curry paste
- 28g soy sauce
- 15g brown sugar
- 15g lime juice
- 21g chopped cilantro
- 28g vegetable oil
- Some salt, to taste

Method to cook:

1. In a large frying pan, flame the vegetable oil over moderate flame. Include the onion, garlic, and ginger, and prepare till softened.
2. Include the red and yellow bell peppers and prepare for some time till slightly softened.
3. Sprinkle red curry paste and prepare for another minute.
4. Include the coconut milk, peanut butter, soy sauce, brown sugar, and lime juice in the tray. Stir to mix.

5. Include the shrimp to the tray and prepare till they are pink and prepared for about 3-5 minutes.
6. Season the curry with some salt to taste.
7. Serve the curry over rice and garnish with cilantro.

Nutritional information (per serving):

Calories: 375, Amino acid level: 27g, Starchs: 15g, Fat: 25g, Fibre: 4g, Sugar: 8g

SEAFOOD GUMBO

Composition time: 5 minutes

Complete time: 35 minutes

Serving: 2

Components used:

- 43g vegetable oil
- 43g flour
- 1 large onion
- 2 green bell peppers
- 3 stalks celery
- 4 cloves garlic, minced
- 1 can dice tomatoes, drained
- 48oz seafood or chicken broth
- 15g Cajun seasoning
- 1.42g cayenne pepper
- 1 pound Andouille sausage, sliced
- 1 pound medium shrimp, peeled and deveined
- 1 pound crabmeat, picked over for shells
- 21g parsley
- Salt and freshly ground pepper, to taste
- Cooked rice, for serving

Method to cook:

1. In a large Dutch cook stove or heavy pot, flame the oil over a moderate flame. Include all-purpose flour and whisk constantly for 20-25 minutes or till the roux turns a dark reddish-brown color.
2. Include the onion, bell peppers, celery, and garlic to the roux and prepare till the vegetables are soft, about 10 minutes.
3. Include the diced tomatoes, broth, Cajun seasoning, and cayenne pepper to the pot and shake to mix. Boil the better and prepare for 1 hour.
4. Include the sliced sausage, shrimp, and crabmeat in the pot and finely cook for extra 10-15 minutes, or till the seafood is cooked through.

5. Include the chopped parsley and season with salt and freshly ground pepper to taste.
6. Serve over cooked rice.

Nutrient facts: This recipe makes about 8 servings. Each serving contains approximately:

- Calories: 421
- Fatty acids: 26g
- Soaked Fatty acids: 5g
- Lipids level: 165mg
- Salt: 1325mg
- Total Starch: 12g
- Whole Fibre: 2g
- Sugars: 4g
- Amino acid level: 35g

MUSSELS & CRAB

Composition time: 10 minutes

Complete time: 10 minutes

Serving: 2

Components used:

- 2 pounds of mussels, cleaned and debearded
- 1 pound of crab meat, cooked and picked
- 15g of olive oil
- 15g of butter
- 1 onion
- 2 cloves of garlic, minced
- 1 red bell pepper
- 85g of white wine
- 85g of chicken broth
- 43g of heavy cream
- 15g of cornstarch
- Salt
- Chopped parsley for garnish

Method to cook:

1. In a large pot or Dutch cook stove, flame the olive oil and butter over moderate flame. Include the chopped onion, garlic, and red bell pepper and prepare till softened, about 5 minutes.

2. Include the white wine and chicken broth in the pot and bring them to a seethe.

3. Include the cleaned and debearded mussels in the pot and cover it with a lid. Cook for 5-7 minutes or till the mussels have opened. Discard any mussels that have not opened.

4. In a pot, mix and mix the heavy cream and cornstarch. Include the crab meat in the pot, then pour in the heavy cream batter. Stir to mix.

5. Cook for another 2-3 minutes, till the sauce, has thickened slightly.

6. Season with Salt.

7. Serve hot, garnished with chopped parsley.

Nutritional information (per serving):

Calories: 415, Fat: 20g, Starchs: 14g, Fibre: 1g, Amino acid level: 36g, Salt: 1236mg

PEACH SALMON

Composition time: 10 minutes

Complete time: 10 minutes

Serving: 2

Components used:

- 4 salmon fillets
- Salt and ground pepper to taste
- 21g peach preserves
- 21g honey
- 21g soy sauce
- 2 cloves garlic, minced
- 15g fresh ginger, grated
- 15g rice vinegar
- 15g sesame oil
- Sliced peaches and green onions for garnish

Method to cook:

1. Warm your cook stove to 375°F (190°C). Line a baking sheet with baking paper or lightly oil with spray oil.
2. Season salmon fillets with salt and ground pepper to taste.
3. In a pot, mix and mix peach preserves, honey, soy sauce, garlic, ginger, rice vinegar, and sesame oil.
4. Place salmon fillets on the baking sheet and brush them generously with the peach glaze.
5. Bake for 12-15 minutes or till the salmon is cooked through and flakes easily with a fork.
6. Garnish with sliced peaches and green onions before eating.

Nutritional information (per serving): Calories: 327 Fatty acids: 14g Soaked Fatty acids: 2g Lipids level:

78mg Salt: 877mg Total Starch: 20g Whole Fibre: 0g Sugar: 18g Amino acid level: 28g

GRILLED TUNA FILLETS WITH CAPRESE

Composition time: 10 minutes

Complete time: 10 minutes

Serving: 2

Components used:

- 4 tuna fillets
- 15g olive oil
- Salt
- 2 large tomatoes, sliced
- 8oz fresh mozzarella cheese, sliced
- 43g fresh basil leaves
- Balsamic glaze (optional)

Method to cook:

1. Warm the grill to a moderate flame.
2. Brush both sides of tuna fillets with olive oil and season with some salt.
3. Grill tuna fillets for 3-4 minutes on each side or till the desired doneness.
4. In the meantime, assemble the Caprese by layering tomato, mozzarella, and basil leaves on a serving platter.
5. Top the Caprese with grilled tuna fillets and sprinkle with balsamic glaze if desired.
6. Serve quickly.

Nutrients facts (1 tuna fillet with Caprese):

Calories: 303 kcal, Starchs: 5g, Amino acid level: 41g, Fat: 12g, Soaked Fatty acids: 4g, Lipids level: 92mg, Salt: 443mg, Potassium: 591mg, Fibre: 1g, Sugar: 3g

TERIYAKI FISH

Composition time: 10 minutes

Complete time: 10 minutes

Serving: 2

Components used:

- 4 (6-ounce) skinless, boneless fish fillets (such as salmon or halibut)
- 21g low-sodium soy sauce

- 21g water
- 28.3g honey
- 28.3g rice vinegar
- 15g grated fresh ginger
- 15g cornstarch
- 1.42g garlic powder
- 1.42g onion powder
- 1.42g ground pepper
- 15g canola oil
- 1 green onion, sliced

Method to cook:

1. Warm the grill to a moderate flame.
2. In a cast iron pan, mix and mix the soy sauce, water, honey, rice vinegar, and ginger. Bring to a seethe over moderate flame.
3. In a different dish, mix and mix the cornstarch, garlic powder, onion powder, and ground pepper. Slowly include the cornstarch batter in the soy sauce batter, constantly whisking till the brew thickens.
4. Brush the fish fillets with canola oil and grill for 5-7 minutes per side or till cooked through.
5. Brush the teriyaki sauce onto the cooked fish fillets and sprinkle with green onions before eating.

Nutrients facts (1 fillet with sauce):

Calories: 290, Fatty acids: 12g, Soaked Fatty acids: 1.5g, Lipids level: 60mg, Salt: 560mg, Total Starch level: 15g, Whole Fibre: 0g, Sugars: 12g, Amino acid level: 28g

BARBEQUED FRYING PAN SALMON

Composition time: 10 minutes

Complete time: 20 minutes

Difficulty Level: Easy

Serving: 2

Components used:

- 4 salmon fillets
- 43g soy sauce
- 21g honey
- 28.3g olive oil
- 2 cloves garlic, minced
- 4.2g grated fresh ginger
- 2.84g ground pepper
- 1.42g red pepper flakes
- 2 green onions, thinly sliced

Method to cook:

1. Warm your grill to a moderate flame.
2. In a pot, mix and mix the soy sauce, honey, olive oil, garlic, ginger, ground pepper, and red pepper flakes.
3. Put the salmon fillets in a shallow dish or a large resealable plastic bag. Sprinkle marinade over the salmon, making sure each fillet is coated evenly. Wrap the tray or seal the bag and marinate the salmon for up to 30 minutes or up to 2 hours in the refrigerator.
4. Take off the salmon from the marinade and discard the leftover marinade.
5. Place a large frying pan on the grill grates and let it flame up for 2-3 minutes.
6. Put the salmon fillets on the tray, skin-side down. Cook the salmon for about 4-5 minutes per side or till the internal temperature of the salmon reaches 145°F (63°C) on an instant-read thermometer.
7. Take off the salmon from the tray and move it to a serving plate. Sprinkle the sliced green onions over the salmon and serve them quickly.

Nutrients facts (1 salmon fillet): Calories: 375 Fatty acids: 18g Soaked Fatty acids: 3g Lipids level: 80mg Salt: 1412mg Total Starch: 19g Whole Fibre: 0g Glucose: 17g Amino acid level: 33g

CORN-STIR FRIED SHRIMPS

Composition time: 5 minutes

Complete time: 35 minutes

Serving: 2

Components used:

- 1 pound large shrimp, peeled and deveined
- 15g cornstarch
- 1.42g salt
- 1.42g ground pepper
- 1.42g paprika
- 1.42g garlic powder
- 28.3g vegetable oil
- 1 red bell pepper
- 1 green bell pepper
- 1 small onion
- 85g corn kernels (fresh or frozen)
- 2 cloves garlic, minced
- 21g chicken or vegetable broth
- 28.3g soy sauce
- 15g honey

- 15g cornstarch
- 2 green onions

Method to cook:

1. In a pot, add the shrimp, 15g cornstarch, salt, ground pepper, paprika, and garlic powder. Mix till the shrimp are coated evenly.

2. Flame the vegetable oil in a large frying pan over moderate flame. Include the shrimp and prepare for 2-3 minutes on each side till pink and prepared through. Take off the shrimp from the tray and set it aside.

3. In the same frying pan, include the red and green bell peppers, onion, corn, and garlic. Cook for 3-4 minutes till the vegetables are very soft.

4. In a pot, mix and mix the chicken or vegetable broth, soy sauce, honey, and 15g cornstarch.

5. Sprinkle sauce into the tray with the vegetables and shake to mix. Cook for 1-2 minutes till the sauce thickens.

6. Include the cooked shrimp back on the tray and toss to coat with the sauce.

7. Garnish with chopped green onions and serve quickly.

Nutritional information (per serving):

Calories: 277, Fatty acids: 10g, Soaked Fatty acids: 1g, Lipids level: 221mg, Salt: 1093mg, Total Starch: 20g, Whole Fibre: 2g, Sugars: 8g, Amino acid level: 28g, Calcium: 119mg, Iron: 3mg

Note: This recipe serves 4

BROCHETTE OYSTERS

Composition time: 5 minutes

Complete time: 30 minutes

Difficulty Level: Easy

Serving: 2

Components used:

- 6 mushrooms.
- 6 big oysters
- A stick of butter (optional)

- Slices of lemon (optional)

Method to cook:

- For this, you'll either need metal skewers or you'll need to plan ahead and soak 6 bamboo skewers in water for a few hours before you start cooking.
- Simply skewer a piece of bacon at the end of the skewer and then a mushroom. Fold the strip of bacon back over, skewer it again, then add an oyster, fold, and skewer the bacon again.
- Put the skewers on a broiler pan and broil them for approximately 10 minutes on Low, near the fire.

Nutrients facts: 289 calories, 18 g fatty acid, 17 g starch, 19 g Amino acid

Glycemic Index: Low

CRAB BISQUE

Composition time: 5 minutes

Complete time: 45 minutes

Difficulty Level: Easy

Serving: 2

Components used:

- 2-pound crab meat
- 1 c. seafood stock
- 2 chopped onions
- A celery stalk four big carrots
- 1 chopped red bell pepper
- chopped garlic cloves
- 43g tomatoes, smashed
- 28.3g tomato paste
- A quarter cup of butter
- Avocado oil (4.2g)
- A half cup of cream
- Bay leaves (two)
- Spices and herbs Components used:
- 8.4g seasoning (old bay)
- 4.2g dried thyme
- Smoked paprika (14 teaspoons)
- 2 chopped tomatoes
- 1 cilantro stalk
- 28g. extra virgin olive oil
- 4.2g dried thyme
- 4.2g chili powder

Method to cook:

- Mix the surface ingredients together and leave aside.
- Soften the butter in the Instant Pot with the oil and bay leaf using the cook mode.
- Cook for 2 minutes after adding the onions.
- Cook for 1 minute after adding the garlic (till aromatic.)
- Cook for 2-3 minutes after adding the herbs and seasoning ingredients, celery, carrots, and bell pepper.
- Mix the fresh tomatoes, crab meat, tomato paste, and broth in a big dish.
- Close and lock the lid.
- Change the vent's setting to Sealing.
- Cook for 12-15 minutes on high.
- When the timer dings, allow the steam to go normally.
- Take off the cover.
- Sprinkle cream till well mixed.
- Mix till smooth, either with an immersion mixer or with a conventional mixer.

Nutrients facts: 301 calories, 13 g fatty acid, 16 g starch, 24 g Amino acid

Glycemic Index: Low

TILAPIA & ZUCCHINI NOODLES

Composition time: 10 minutes

Complete time: 20 minutes

Serving: 2

Components used:

- 4 tilapia fillets
- 2 large zucchinis, spiralized into noodles
- 28g olive oil
- 15g minced garlic
- 15g paprika
- Salt
- Lemon corners for serving

Method to cook:

1. Warm your grill or grill pan to moderate flame.
2. Rub the tilapia fillets with 15g of olive oil and season with salt, pepper, and paprika.
3. Grill the tilapia for 4-5 minutes per side or till the fish is cooked through and flakes easily with a fork.

4. While the fish is grilling, flame the leftover 15g of olive oil in a large pan over moderate flame.
5. Include the minced garlic to the tray and cook for 1-2 minutes or till fragrant.
6. Include the zucchini noodles to the tray and cook for 2-3 minutes, or till the noodles are very soft.
7. Season the zucchini noodles with Salt.
8. Serve the grilled tilapia fillets on top of the zucchini noodles, with lemon corners on the side for squeezing over the fish.

Nutrients facts (based on 4 servings): Calories: 224 Fatty acids: 10g Soaked Fatty acids: 2g Lipids level: 57mg Salt: 71mg Total Starch: 5g Whole Fibre: 1g Sugar: 2g Amino acid level: 30g

SWEET GARLIC SHRIMP

Composition time: 0 minutes

Complete time: 35 minutes

Serving: 2

Components used:

- 1 lb shrimp, peeled and deveined
- 3 cloves garlic, minced
- 15g olive oil
- 28g honey
- 15g soy sauce
- 15g rice vinegar
- 1/28g red pepper flakes
- Some salt, to taste
- Chopped green onions for garnish

Method to cook:

1. In a pot, mix, and mix garlic, olive oil, honey, soy sauce, rice vinegar, red pepper flakes, and some salt.

2. Put the shrimp in a pot and sprinkle marinade over the shrimp. Toss well to coat.

3. Cover and marinate for up to 30 minutes in the fridge.

4. Warm the cook stove to 400°F.

5. Line a baking sheet with baking paper.

6. Arrange the shrimp on the baking sheet and pour any remaining marinade over the shrimp.

7. Bake for 8-10 minutes or till the shrimp is cooked through and pink.

8. Garnish with chopped green onions.

Nutritional Information (per serving):

- Calories: 173
- Fat: 4g
- Starches: 12g
- Fibre: 0g
- Amino acid level: 22g
- Sugar: 10g
- Salt: 584mg

CRISPY FISH FINGERS

Composition time: 10 minutes

Complete time: 20 minutes

Serving: 2

Components used:

- 1 pound white fish fillets (such as cod or haddock)
- 43g flour
- 2.84g salt
- 1.42g ground pepper
- 2 eggs, beaten
- 85g panko breadcrumbs
- 2.84g paprika
- Vegetable oil, for frying

Method to cook:

1. Slice the fish fillets into fingers, about 1 inch wide by 3 inches long.

2. In a shallow dish, add all purpose flour, salt, and ground pepper.

3. In another shallow dish, beat the eggs.

4. In a third shallow dish, add the trayko breadcrumbs and paprika.

5. Dredge each fish finger in all-purpose flour batter, shaking off any excess. Dip the fish in the beaten eggs, then coat it with the breadcrumb batter. Press the breadcrumbs onto the fish to make sure they adhere.

6. Flame about 1/2 inch of vegetable oil in a large frying pan over moderate flame.

7. Fry the fish fingers in the hot oil till golden brown and crispy, about 3-4 minutes per side. Drain on paper towels. Serve with your favorite dipping sauce.

Nutritional Information (per serving): Calories: 348 Fatty acids: 11.9g Soaked Fatty acids: 2.1g Lipids level: 139mg Salt: 590mg Total Starch level:

26.4g Whole Fibre: 1.4g Sugar: 1.4g Amino acid level: 32.6g

TUNA SALAD WITH LEMON ZEST

Composition time: 0 minutes

Complete time: 15 minutes

Serving: 2

Components used:

- 2 cans of tuna in water, drained
- 21g of mayonnaise
- 21g of yogurt
- 28.3g of lemon juice
- 15g of lemon zest
- 1.42g of salt
- 1.42g of ground pepper
- Optional additions: diced celery, diced onion, diced cucumber, fresh parsley

Method to cook:

1. In a pot, mix the drained tuna, mayonnaise, Greek yogurt, lemon juice, lemon zest, and some salt till well mixed.
2. If desired, Pour any additional ingredients such as diced celery, onion, cucumber, or parsley.
3. Serve the tuna salad on top of a bed of greens, in a sandwich, or with crackers.

Nutritional information (per serving):

Calories: 190, Fatty acids: 10g, Soaked Fatty acids: 2g, Lipids level: 42mg, Salt: 460mg, Total Starch level: 3g, Whole Fibre: 0g, Sugars: 2g, Amino acid level: 22g

CITRUS SALMON

Composition time: 10 minutes

Complete time: 10 minutes

Serving: 2

Components used:

- 4 salmon fillets
- 1 orange
- 1 lemon
- 1 lime
- 2 cloves garlic, minced
- 28.3g olive oil
- Salt

Method to cook:

1. Warm your cook stove to 400°F.
2. Slice the orange, lemon, and lime into thin slices.
3. In a pot, mix the minced garlic, olive oil, and some salt.
4. Lay out four pieces of foil or baking paper, large enough to wrap around each salmon fillet.
5. Place one salmon fillet on each piece of foil or baking paper.
6. Brush each salmon fillet with the garlic and olive oil batter.
7. Top each salmon fillet with several slices of citrus fruit.
8. Wrap the sheet or baking paper around each salmon fillet, creating a packet.
9. Put the packets on a baking sheet and prepare for 12-15 minutes, till the salmon is cooked through and flakes easily with a fork.
10. Serve the salmon hot, with extra citrus slices for garnish.

Nutrients facts:

- Calories: 290
- Fatty acids: 16g
- Soaked Fatty acids: 3g
- Lipids level: 85mg
- Salt: 77mg
- Total Starch level: 4g
- Whole Fibre: 1g
- Sugars: 2g
- Amino acid level: 30g

INSTANT MUSSELS

Composition time: 10 minutes

Complete time: 10 minutes

Serving: 2

Components used:

- 28.3g unsalted butter
- 2 green onions
- 4 garlic cloves, minced
- 1-28g broth (seafood)
- Mussels, 2 lbs., cleaned
- 1 lemon, to serve
- 21g fresh parsley/thyme

Method to cook:

- Wash and debar mussels; discard any mussels with fractured shells or shells that do not close.
- In the Instant Pot, soften the butter in the cook mode.
- Include the onions and prepare, mixing regularly, till transparent.
- Include the garlic and finely cook for 1 minute, or till fragrant.
- Pour in the broth and whisk everything together.
- Include the mussels and mix well.
- Close and lock the lid.
- Change the vent's setting to Sealing.
- Cook for 5 minutes under high pressure.
- When the timer dings, allow the steam to go normally.
- Take off the cover.
- Move the mussels to a plate to serve.

Nutrients facts: 329 calories, 18 g fatty acid, 17 g starch, 19 g Amino acid

SHRIMP RICE WITH PINEAPPLE

Composition time: 5 minutes

Complete time: 35 minutes

Serving: 2

Components used:

- 85g uncooked rice
- 1 lb large shrimp, peeled and deveined
- 1 red bell pepper
- 1 yellow onion
- 1 garlic clove, minced
- 85g pineapple small pieces
- 28.3g soy sauce
- 15g brown sugar
- 15g rice vinegar
- 15g vegetable oil
- Salt and ground pepper to taste
- Chopped cilantro for garnish

Method to cook:

1. Cook the rice according to package instructions and set aside.
2. In a large frying pan or wok, flame the vegetable oil over moderate flame.
3. Include the onion and prepare for 2-3 minutes till soft.
4. Include the garlic and prepare for an extra minute.

5. Include the red bell pepper and prepare for another 2-3 minutes till slightly softened.
6. Include the shrimp and prepare for 2-3 minutes till pink and prepared through.
7. Include the pineapple in small pieces and prepare for an extra minute.
8. In a pot, mix and mix the soy sauce, brown sugar, and rice vinegar.
9. Sprinkle sauce over the shrimp and vegetables and shake to coat.
10. Include the cooked rice in the tray and shake to mix.
11. Season with salt and ground pepper to taste.
12. Garnish with chopped cilantro before eating.

Nutritional Information (per serving):

Calories: 387 kcal, Amino acid level: 26g, Fat: 5g, Starchs: 61g, Fibre: 3g, Sugar: 12g, Salt: 699mg

PARMESAN BAKED TILAPIA

Composition time: 10 minutes

Complete time: 10 minutes

Difficulty Level: Easy

Serving: 2

Components used:

- 6-ounce tilapia fillets, cleaned and patted dry
- 28g. mayonnaise (mild)
- a third of a cup of panko breadcrumbs
- 21g grated Parmesan cheese 15g grated lemon zest
- 28g. fresh parsley, freshly chopped
- 15g. rapeseed oil
- 2.84g oregano leaves, dried
- paprika, 2.84g
- salt (1.42g)
- 8 slices of moderate tomato

Method to cook:

- Warm the cook stove to 400 degrees Fahrenheit. Meanwhile, brush the mayonnaise over the tilapia on a foil-lined baking sheet sprayed with spray oil. In a pot, mix the leftover ingredients. Stir with a fork till crumbly, then heap on top of the fillets.
- Bake for 18–20 minutes or till the center of the fish is opaque. Serve with 2 tomato slices on the side.

Nutrients facts: 292 calories, 13 g fatty acid, 16 g starch, 24 g Amino acid

Glycemic Index: Low

CHINESE STEAMED FISH

Composition time: 0 minutes

Complete time: 40 minutes

Difficulty Level: Easy

Serving: 2

Components used:

- 12 fluid oz (340 g) fillets of fish
- A quarter-cup (28 ml) sherry (dry)
- 15g of oil (15 ml) sauce de soda
- tbsp. gingerroot, grated
- 1 smashed garlic clove or 2.84g minced garlic
- 1 1/28.3g sesame oil, toasted
- 1 or 2 minced scallions (optional)

Method to cook:

- Put the fish fillets on a heavy-duty tin sheet and fold the sides up to create a lip.
- Mix the sherry, soy sauce, gingerroot, garlic, and sesame oil in a pot.
- In a big frying pan, place a rack—a cake-chilling rack works well. Turn the flame to high and pour approximately 1/4 inch (6 mm) of water into the bottom of the tray.
- Put the sheet on the rack with the fish on it. Sprinkle sherry batter over the fish with care. Close the lid securely on the tray.
- Cook for 5–7 minutes or till the fish readily flakes. If desired, garnish with finely chopped onions.

Nutrients facts: 292 calories, 13 g fatty acid, 16 g starch, 24 g Amino acid

Glycemic Index: Low

PRAWN DELIGHT

Composition time: 10 minutes

Complete time: 10 minutes

Difficulty Level: Easy

Serving: 2

Components used:

- 4 tbsp. extra virgin olive oil
- 500 grams of medium raw prawns

- 6-8 garlic cloves, minced
- 21g fresh lemon juice 85g chicken stock
- 15g. additional chopped parsley (14 cups)
- seasoning with some salt
- 4 slices of lemon (lemon has 2.5g of stevia per 100g)

Method to cook:

- In a big fry pan, flame the oil. Cook prawns in a frying pan over low-moderate flame till pink, about 2-3 minutes.
- Toss in the garlic. Cook for 30 seconds, mixing regularly. Place prawns on a serving dish or tray.
- In a very low cook stove, cover and keep the prawns warm.
- In a frying pan, combine chicken stock, lemon juice, wine, 14 cup parsley, and spices; bring to a seethe. Boil till the sauce has been reduced by half.
- Sprinkle the sauce over the prawns and garnish with the leftover tbsp. parsley. Serve with salad greens that have been freshly prepared.

Nutrients facts: 292 calories, 13 g fatty acid, 16 g starch, 24 g Amino acid

Glycemic Index: Low

COCONUT CRUSTED FLOUNDER

Composition time: 10 minutes

Complete time: 10 minutes

Difficulty Level: Easy

Serving: 2

Components used:

- Some salt (or Vege-Sal) 43g (63 g) coconut powder
- Three eggs
- 1 and 1/2 pound (680 g) fillet of flounder
- 1 pound of butter, split
- A single lime
- 4 tbsp. (16 g) fresh parsley, minced

Method to cook:

- Apply a dab of nonstick spray oil to your big, heavy pan and place it over a moderate flame to flame.
- Mix the coconut powder and some salt on a plate (about 1.42g each).

- Beat the eggs with a tablespoon (15 ml) of water on a different dish with a rim.
- Half of the butter should be softened in the tray.
- On all sides, dip each fillet in the egg, then the coconut powder, then the egg, then all-purpose flour. Put them in the softened butter!
- Allow your fish to cook for 4 to 5 minutes on each side or till crispy brown. When you flip the fish, add a bit more butter if necessary. Plate it when it's brown on both sides.
- Now include the leftover butter in the flamed pan and allow it to soften and brown. Over the flounder fillets, sprinkle browned butter. Serve with a slice of lime and parsley on top.

Nutrients facts: 292 calories, 13 g fatty acid, 16 g starch, 24 g Amino acid

Glycemic Index: Low

ROASTED SALMON WITH DILLED YOGHURT

Composition time: 10 minutes

Complete time: 40 minutes

Difficulty Level: Easy

Serving: 2

Components used:

- 43g sliced tomatoes
- 1 1/4 pound fillet of salmon
- 28g. canola seed oil
- 2.84g oregano leaves, dried
- a quarter teaspoon of salt, divided
- a quarter teaspoon of ground pepper, split
- 21g cucumber, peeled and coarsely chopped
- 1 2.84gs capers, drained
- 28g nonfat Greek yogurt
- 15g mayonnaise (light)
- 15g fresh dill
- 2 sliced moderate tomatoes

Method to cook:

- Warm the cook stove to 350 degrees Fahrenheit. Meanwhile, lay the salmon on a foil-lined baking sheet, skin side down. Using the oregano, 1/8 teaspoon salt, and 1/8 teaspoon ground pepper, brush the oil over the fish. In a pot, mix the other ingredients (excluding the fresh tomatoes).

- 2. Bake the salmon for 18–20 minutes or till the middle is opaque. Serve the caper batter beside the salmon, on top of the fresh tomatoes.

Nutrients facts: 292 calories, 13 g fatty acid, 16 g starch, 24 g Amino acid

Glycemic Index: Low

GARLIC MOCK LOBSTER

Composition time: 0 minutes

Complete time: 15 minutes

Difficulty Level: Easy

Serving: 2

Components used:

- 1 1/28.3g butter (21 g)
- 6oz 2.84g minced garlic
- 1 smashed garlic clove (170 g) fillet of monkfish.

Method to cook:

- Put the butter on a platter that can be microwaved. Microwave for 30 seconds at 70% power or till softened. In a pot, add the garlic and butter.
- Put the monkfish in the butter and flip it over so that all sides are coated. Microwave-safe plastic wrap should be used to wrap the fish.
- At 50% power, microwave for 1 1/2 minutes. ReWrap the fish by turning it over and wrapping it in plastic wrap.
- Continue to nuke for another 30 seconds at 50% power. Take off the plastic wrap and check for doneness after a minute (or a minute or two longer if you're cooking another serving). Recover if required, then give it another 30 seconds or so before eating.

Nutrients facts: 292 calories, 13 g fatty acid, 16 g starch, 24 g Amino acid

Glycemic Index: Low

BASIC CHICKEN WINGS

Composition time: 0 minutes

Complete time: 25 minutes

Difficulty Level: Easy

Serving: 6

Components used:

- 1/2 serving of all-purpose low-carb baking mix
- 28g. cayenne pepper
- 4.2g cayenne
- 28g. mustard seed (yellow)
- 8.4g of salt
- 12-16 pieces of chicken wings

Method to cook:

- Set the cook stove's temperature to 450 degrees Fahrenheit.
- Clean the chicken wings by rinsing them.
- Use tin sheet to line a baking pan. Using nonstick frying spray, coat the tray.
- Add the baking mix, chili powder, cayenne pepper, mustard seed, and some salt in a Ziploc bag. Fill the bag with the wings. To coat the chicken wings with spice, massage them through the bag.
- Place on a baking sheet. Cook for 30-35 minutes, mixing periodically, or till golden brown.

Nutrients facts: 299 calories, 13 g fatty acid, 15 g starch, 21 g Amino acid

Glycemic Index: Low

CHICKEN & SHRIMP IN THAI STYLE

Composition time: 0 minutes

Complete time: 30 minutes

Difficulty Level: Moderate

Serving: 2

Components used:

- 2 chicken breasts, boneless and skinless
- 6 quarts (1.4 liters) of water
- 1 peeled and chopped small onion
- 1 leaf of bay
- 2 parsley sprigs
- ½ tsp of thyme
- ¼ tsp of pepper
- 1 crushed garlic clove
- a couple of tablespoons (4 g) coriander
- 1 and a half teaspoons of chili powder
- 15g of oil (15 ml)
- Shrimp, 1/2 pound (225 g)
- 6 scallions, with tops, sliced
- 400g (140 g) sliced mushrooms,
- 28g fresh cilantro

Method to cook:

- Slice the meat into strips. Water is placed in a large cast iron pan halfway. Water, an onion, a bay leaf, parsley, thyme, and some salt should be added.
- Bring the fresh water to a seethe. Lower the flame and prepare slowly, covered, for 1 hour. Strain broth into a cast iron pan.
- Mix garlic, coriander, chili powder, and soy sauce. Pourto broth. Bring the fresh water to a seethe.
- Add chicken, shrimp, and mushrooms. Cook slowly, covered, for about 5 minutes, till the shrimp turns pink and the chicken is very soft.
- Pour scallions and fresh cilantro. Take off and discard the bay leaf. Serve in dishes over or with rice.

Nutrients facts: 384 calories, 13 g fatty acid, 14 g starch, 21 g Amino acid

Glycemic Index: Low

CHICKEN CURRY

Composition time: 10 minutes

Complete time: 50 minutes

Difficulty Level: Easy

Serving: 2

Components used:

- 2 Pounds. sliced chicken
- 28g. extra virgin olive oil
- four (4) green 2 garlic cloves
- 2 small peppers
- finely chopped onions
- finely chopped tomatoes
- 1 quart of water

- Lemon juice, 15g.
- 43g fresh cilantro
- 2 cardamoms (black)
- bay leaves (two)
- 4 garlic cloves
- 8.4g ground pepper
- a third of a teaspoon of cumin seeds
- 28.3g powdered coriander
- 2.84g cayenne pepper

Method to cook:

- In the Instant Pot, use the cook mode to warm the oil.
- Cook for 20 seconds after adding the entire spices.
- Cook for 5 minutes after adding the onions, green chili, ginger, and garlic (till they turn golden brown.)
- Cook for another 4 minutes after adding the fresh tomatoes.
- Include the chicken and finely cook for another 2-4 minutes.
- Add the fresh water and the other ingredients to a pot.
- Scrape the bottom of the tray and deglaze it.
- Close and lock the lid.
- Change the vent's setting to Sealing.
- Cook for 6 minutes under high pressure.
- Quickly release the steam when the timer sounds.
- Take off the cover.
- Squeeze the lemon juice into the brew.
- Move to a serving plate and garnish with cilantro.
- Put the food on the table.

Nutrients facts: 292 calories, 13 g fatty acid, 16 g starch, 24 g Amino acid

Glycemic Index: Low

CHICKEN THIGHS & ARTICHOKE HEARTS

Composition time: 10 minutes

Complete time: 15 minutes

Difficulty Level: Moderate

Serving: 2

Components used:

- 85g olive oil
- 6 boneless, skinless chicken thighs

- 1 (14-ounce) can of artichoke hearts, drained
- 1 onion, diced
- 43g bone broth
- 4.2g salt
- 4.2g freshly crushed ground pepper
- 1 lemon juice

Method to cook:

- Rewarm the cook stove to 400 degrees Fahrenheit.
- In a large cast iron pan, warm the olive oil over moderate Warm. Cook for 4 minutes, or till the chicken is beautifully browned on the bottom.
- After the chicken has browned, turn it over and sprinkle artichokes, onion, stock, and some salt.
- Bake the tray for 40 minutes, or till the chicken is cooked through, in a rewarmed cook stove.
- Take the tray out of the cook stove and sprinkle lemon juice all over it. Serve quickly.

Nutrients facts: 380 calories, 13 g fatty acid, 16 g starch, 24 g Amino acid

Glycemic Index: Low

CHICKEN NOODLES WITH PEANUT SAUCE

Composition time: 10 minutes

Complete time: 30 minutes

Difficulty Level: Easy

Serving: 2

Components used:

- Spaghetti, 8 oz. (225 g)
- 43g creamy peanut butter (130 g)
- a quarter-cup (30 ml) Dick's Soy Sauce with Low Sodium (see recipe in chapter 2)
- 4.2g grated gingerroot
- a half-cup (120 ml) chicken broth with minimal sodium
- a quarter pound (115 g) of sprouted beans
- 1 pound (455 g) boneless skinless chicken breast 85g (150 g) red bell peppers, cut 2 green onions, sliced

Method to cook:

- Prepare the spaghetti. In a cast iron pan, mix peanut butter, soy sauce, and gingerroot. Pour in the chicken broth.

- Mix the spaghetti, bean sprouts, bell pepper, and onion in a big dish. Toss. Chicken should be sliced into thin pieces. Stir-fry till the meat is no longer pink. Toss into the spaghetti sauce.

Nutrients facts: 238 calories, 13 g fatty acid, 16 g starch, 24 g Amino acid

Glycemic Index: Low

CHICKEN MEATBALLS WITH MARINA AND BEAN SPROUTS

Composition time: 10 minutes

Complete time: 30 minutes

Difficulty Level: Easy

Serving: 2

Components used:

- 1 pound ground chicken
- 21g extra virgin olive oil
- 400g chopped broccoli
- 1 (24-ounce) jar of low-carb marinara sauce
- 1 (12-ounce) bag of bean sprouts

Method to cook:

- From the ground chicken, form 12 meatballs.
- In a large frying pan set over a moderate flame, warm the oil. For around 8 minutes, cook the meatballs while flipping them continuously. In a pot, add the marinara sauce and broccoli. Cook for 30 minutes, cover, and Lower flame to a low warm.
- Include the bean sprouts, increase the flame to medium, and finely cook for extra 15 minutes with the lid off. Serve right away.

Nutrients facts: 230 calories, 13 g fatty acid, 16 g starch, 24 g Amino acid

Glycemic Index: Low

CHICKEN WINGS WITH BUFFALO SAUCE

Composition time: 10 minutes

Complete time: 30 minutes

Difficulty Level: Moderate

Serving: 2

Components used:

- A dozen big eggs (whole)
- Apple cider vinegar, 85g
- 28g extra virgin olive oil
- 4.2g powdered garlic
- 1.42g cayenne pepper
- 4.2g celery salt
- 2-pound boned and skinned chicken wing
- Mayonnaise (16 tbsp.)
- 43g cultured sour cream
- scallions (medium)
- 43g crumbled blue cheese
- 1 lemon juice (fluidoz)
- 2 minced garlic cloves

Method to cook:

- Warm the cook stove to 440°F.
- Mix the egg, vinegar, olive oil, salt, pepper, garlic powder, celery salt, and cayenne in a pot.
- Wrap the chicken wings in the marinade and lay them on a big baking sheet.
- Bake for 30 minutes (or till the wings are crisp); flip and brush with marinade several times.
- Sauce for dipping
- Chop scallions and garlic cloves.
- Set aside a batter of mayonnaise, sour cream, blue cheese, scallions, lemon juice, and garlic.
- Serve the wings with the dipping sauce as soon as they come out of the cook stove.

Nutrients facts: 369 calories, 13 g fatty acid, 16 g starch, 27 g Amino acid, Glycemic Index: Low

CHICKEN FRIED RICE

Composition time: 10 minutes

Complete time: 60 minutes

Difficulty Level: Easy

Serving: 2

Components used:

- one pound (455 g) chicken breasts, boneless and skinless
- a half teaspoon of cornstarch
- a pinch of white pepper
- 85g bean sprouts (50 g)
- 5 tablespoons of oil (75 ml) oil
- 2 gently beaten eggs
- 70 g mushrooms, sliced

- 3 mugs (495 g) rice
- a quarter-cup Soy Sauce
- 2 sliced green onions with tops

Method to cook:

- Slice the chicken into pieces that are 1/4-inch (5 mm) thick. In a pot, add the chicken, cornstarch, and a dash of white pepper.
- The wok should be flameed all the way up. Apply 15 ml of oil (15g) on the sides. Put the eggs in. Cook the eggs till they have thickened but are still liquid, continually mixing. Exit the wok with the eggs. Clean and dry the wok well.
- Reflame the tray and add two teaspoons (30 ml) of oil to the corners. Cook the chicken, mixing continuously, till it becomes white.
- At this point, bean sprouts and mushrooms should be included. Drain the wok's contents after one minute of mixing.
- Wok should be flameed to high before adding 28.3g of oil to coat the sides. For one minute, Sprinkle rice.
- Sprinkle soy sauce after adding it. For 30 seconds, Sprinkle eggs, chicken batter, and green onions.

Nutrients facts: 285 calories, 13 g fatty acid, 16 g starch, 24 g Amino acid

Glycemic Index: Low

SMOKED & SPICY CHICKEN WITH STEW

Composition time: 10 minutes

Complete time: 30 minutes

Difficulty Level: Moderate

Serving: 2

Components used:

- 2 pounds ground chicken
- 2 boneless, skinless chicken thighs, cut into 12-inch dice
- 2 cup chopped onions
- 4 tablespoons minced garlic
- 28.3g smoked paprika
- 15g ground cumin
- 15g dried oregano leaves
- 8.4g fine sea salt
- 4.2g cayenne pepper
- 400g chicken bone broth, homemade or store-bought

- cilantro, lime wcorners or slices

Method to cook:

- In a large soup pot over moderate Warm, add the fat, ground chicken, diced chicken thighs, and onions. Cook for approximately 6 minutes, or till the onions are very soft and the chicken is cooked through.
- Include the garlic, paprika, cumin, oregano, salt, and cayenne to the cast iron pan and prepare, mixing constantly, for another minute. Add the fresh tomatoes, juices, broth, sparkling water, and chocolate in a pot. To allow the flavors to emerge, stew for 10 minutes.

Nutrients facts: 337 calories, 13 g fatty acid, 16 g starch, 24 g Amino acid

Glycemic Index: Low

CHICKEN CASHEW NUT

Composition time: 10 minutes

Complete time: 10 minutes

Difficulty Level: Easy

Serving: 2

Components used:

- 2 boneless, skinless chicken breasts
- 3 teaspoons of oil (45 ml) Soy Sauce
- 15g sherry or rice wine (15 ml)
- 15g cornstarch (8 g)
- 28.3g stevia (9 g)
- 4.2g vinegar (white)
- Vegetable oil, 21g
- 2.84g crushed red pepper
- 3 sliced green onions
- 15g (6 g) minced fresh ginger
- a half-cup (70 g) cashews, unsalted

Method to cook:

- For 30 minutes, prepare the chicken in 15g (15 ml) soy sauce and rice wine. Set aside 8.4g (30 ml) of soy sauce, cornstarch, stevia, and vinegar. In a wok or pan, flame the oil. Cook till black, seasoning with red pepper to taste. Stir-fry the chicken for 2 minutes.
- Take off the chicken from the equation. Sprinkle green onions and ginger for 1 minute. Toss the chicken back into the wok.

- Cook, mixing frequently for 2 minutes; include the soy sauce batter and any residual chicken marinade.
- Toss in the cashews. Cook till the sauce has thickened and is bubbling.

Nutrients facts: 361 calories, 13 g fatty acid, 16 g starch, 24 g Amino acid

Glycemic Index: Low

CHICKEN DRUMSTICKS

Composition time: 10 minutes

Complete time: 10 minutes

Difficulty Level: Easy

Serving: 2

Components used:

- 1 pound of skinned chicken drumsticks on sauce
- 28g. sesame seed oil
- 1/3 gallon of water
- teaspoons apple cider vinegar
- a half cup of stevia
- garlic cloves, minced
- 15g grated ginger
- 28g. crushed red pepper

Method to cook:

- In a pot, combine all of the sauce ingredients.
- Add the chicken and sauce in a zip-lock freezer bag and place in the freezer till totally frozen.
- In the Instant Pot, add the chicken and sauce. Close and lock the lid. Change the vent's setting to Sealing.
- Cook for 15 minutes on high pressure.
- When the timer sounds, allow the steam go naturally for 10-15 minutes. Take off the cover.
- Warm the cook stove to broil and prepare a baking sheet with baking paper.
- Put the drumsticks on a baking sheet after removing them from the Instant Pot. Sprinkle the Instant Pot sauce over the chicken.
- Cook the chicken for 5 minutes on each side under the broiler. Move the tray to a serving plate. Put the food on the table.

Nutrients facts: 292 calories, 13 g fatty acid, 16 g starch, 24 g Amino acid

Glycemic Index: Low

GLAZED CHICKEN WITH VEGETABLES

Composition time: 10 minutes

Complete time: 10 minutes

Difficulty Level: Easy

Serving: 2

Components used:

- 2 shredded boneless chicken breasts
- 1 beaten egg white
- a quarter-cup (1 6 g) cornstarch
- 28.3g chicken broth
- 4.2g vinegar (red wine)
- to taste ground pepper
- a quarter-cup (30 ml) sesame seed oil
- a half-cup (65 g) carrots, sliced
- 4.2g gingerroot
- 85g (71 g) florets of broccoli
- 85g (70 g) mushrooms, sliced
- a quarter cup (60 ml) water
- 1 1/28.3g mustard powder
- 21g sliced scallions (25 g)

Method to cook:

- In a pot, add the first four ingredients with 15g (8 g) of the cornstarch, whisk till smooth, and set aside. In a another dish, add the vinegar, pepper, soy sauce, and chicken broth. Take it out of the equation. Make the oil hot in a wok. For one minute, Sprinkle carrots, ginger, broccoli, and mushrooms.
- Turn the flame down to low and give the chicken broth batter a minute to boil. While the sauce is stewing, add the leftover cornstarch, water, and mustard powder. Flame it up to a medium setting.
- When the sauce starts to boil, include the chicken batter and scallions. Cook the chicken for one minute, or till it is fully white.
- Whisk in the cornstarch batter and stir constantly till the sauce thickens.

Nutrients facts: 299 calories, 13 g fatty acid, 15 g starch, 21 g Amino acid

Glycemic Index: Low

CHICKEN WITH SNOW PEAS

Composition time: 10 minutes

Complete time: 10 minutes

Difficulty Level: Easy

Serving: 2

Components used:

- one pound (455 g) chicken breasts with no bones
- cornstarch, 8.4g (16 g)
- 1 beaten egg white
- 15g of oil (15 ml) sherry
- a quarter teaspoon of white pepper
- 8oz (225 g) chopped mushrooms
- 1 43gs (355 ml) chicken broth
- 15g (6 g) ginger root, sliced
- 5 tbsp. (75 ml) extra virgin olive oil, divided
- 21g (25 g) green onion, sliced
- 21g (25 g) celery slices
- a quarter pound (115 g) peas des neighs
- sliced water chestnuts, 21g (31 g)
- 1 mug (70 g) Napa cabbage, roughly shredded

Method to cook:

- Mix the chicken, 15g (8 g) cornstarch, egg white, sherry, and pepper in a pot. Marinate. 15 minutes of stewing mushrooms in broth. Drain the liquid and set it aside. 8.4g (30 ml) water + remaining cornstarch to dissolve completely, give it a good shake. In a wok or big frying pan, flame 37g (45 ml) olive oil. Cook with the chicken.
- Drain the liquid onto a sieve set over a basin. Toss in the leftover olive oil in the wok. Stir-fry for 2 minutes with onions, celery, snow peas, water chestnuts, mushrooms, and cabbage.
- Take off the ginger from the chicken broth. Bring the fresh water to a seethe. Toss the chicken back into the wok. Pour in the fresh water and cornstarch batter.

Nutrients facts: 317 calories, 13 g fatty acid, 16 g starch, 24 g Amino acid

Glycemic Index: Low

TINGA CHICKEN

Composition time: 10 minutes

Complete time: 10 minutes

Difficulty Level: Easy

Serving: 2

Components used:

- a pound of bone-in, skin-on chicken thighs
- a quarter cup of chopped onions
- 4oz Mexican-style fresh (raw) chorizo
- 1/2 big white onion, sliced
- 15g minced garlic
- 15g fine sea salt
- 1/28g powdered ground pepper
- 1 garlic clove, minced
- 2.84g dried oregano leaves
- 3 cups chopped tomatoes
- 85g husked and diced tomatillos
- 28.3g pureed chipotle
- 1 2.84gs fine sea salt
- 4.2g ground ground pepper
- 1 fresh marjoram sprig
- 1 fresh thyme sprig
- 43g homemade or store-bought chicken bone broth

Method to cook:

- In a large cast iron pan, add the chicken, onions, garlic, some salt, along with 5 cups of water. Bring to a seethe over moderate Warm, then lower to medium and continue to cook for another 20 minutes.
- Move the chicken to a chopping board and set aside. Take off the chicken from the bones with 2 forks and shred it; discard the bones and put aside the shredded chicken.
- Put the chorizo in a large cast-iron pan and crumble it. Put the tray over medium Warm, include the onion and garlic, and prepare, turning often, for approximately 5 minutes, or till the sausage is cooked through. Flip together the shredded chicken, tomatoes, tomatillos, chipotle, salt, pepper, and herbs in a pot. Stew for another 5 minutes before adding the chicken broth and continuing to cook for another 5 minutes.

- Take off the sprigs of marjoram and thyme. Flip with tortillas or lettuce leaves before eating.

Nutrients facts: 316 calories, 13 g fatty acid, 16 g starch, 24 g Amino acid

Glycemic Index: Low

GARLIC CHICKEN WINGS

Composition time: 10 minutes

Complete time: 30 minutes

Difficulty Level: Moderate

Serving: 2

Components used:

- 2 frozen chicken wings
- 85g extra virgin olive oil
- 6 minced garlic cloves
- 1 1/28.3g salt
- 4.2g freshly ground ground pepper

Method to cook:

- Rewarm the cook stove to 400 degrees Fahrenheit. A big baking sheet should be placed on top of a baking rack.
- Flip the frozen wings with the olive oil, garlic, some salt in a pot.
- Put the chicken pieces on the baking sheet on top of the cook stove rack.
- Bake for 1 hour, or till browned and crisp, in a rewarmed cook stove.

Nutrients facts: 318 calories, 13 g fatty acid, 16 g starch, 24 g Amino acid

Glycemic Index: Low

TERIYAKI CHICKEN WITH SESAME

Composition time: 10 minutes

Complete time: 10 minutes

Difficulty Level: Easy

Serving: 2

Components used:

- a quarter-cup Teriyaki Sauce
- 408 500 1 spoonful (15 ml) water
- 2 garlic cloves, minced
- 1.42g ginger powder
- boneless, skinless chicken breasts
- 1.42g roasted sesame seeds

Method to cook:

- In a pot, mix the teriyaki sauce, water, garlic, and ginger for the marinade. Include the chicken and mix well. Allow it rest for 20 minutes, mixing regularly.
- Drain. Accordion-style, thread chicken onto two 0-12-inch (25-30 cm) skewers or four 6-inch (15 cm) skewers.
- Place on a broiler pan's unflameed rack. Broil for 3 minutes at a distance of 4-5 inches (10-13 cm) from the flame source.
- Broil for another 2-3 minutes, or till the chicken is cooked and no longer pink. 2 servings (about)

Nutrients facts: 292 calories, 13 g fatty acid, 16 g starch, 24 g Amino acid

Glycemic Index: Low

CHILI-GARLIC CHICKEN WITH BROCCOLI

Composition time: 10 minutes

Complete time: 30 minutes

Difficulty Level: Moderate

Serving: 2

Components used:

- 6 boneless, skinless chicken breasts
- 1 head broccoli
- 8oz whole mushrooms
- 1 large onion, diced
- 400g bone broth
- 43g coconut aminos
- 5 tablespoons chili-garlic sauce
- 21g avocado oil
- 28.3g fish sauce

Method to cook:

- Flip the chicken, broccoli, mushrooms, onion, bone broth, coconut aminos, chili-garlic sauce, avocado oil, fish sauce, garlic, and ginger together in a slow cooker.
- Cook on low for 6 hours, covered. Serve quickly.

Nutrients facts: 248 calories, 13 g fatty acid, 16 g starch, 24 g Amino acid

Glycemic Index: Low

CHINESE MEATBALLS

Composition time: 10 minutes

Complete time: 10 minutes

Difficulty Level: Easy

Serving: 2

Components used:

- one pound (455 g) chicken breasts, ground
- 6 g sodium-free beef bouillon, 15g.
- a quarter teaspoon of ginger
- 1/8 teaspoon powdered garlic
- a quarter teaspoon of ground pepper
- sherry, 15g (15 ml)
- a single egg

Method to cook:

- Mix all ingredients in a pot.
- Make 1-inch (2 1 12 cm) balls out of the dough. Place in a roasting pan that has been well sprayed with nonstick vegetable oil.
- Roast for 30 to 40 minutes at 176°C (180°C, gas mark 4) till done, turning once.

Nutrients facts: 283 calories, 13 g fatty acid, 16 g starch, 24 g Amino acid

Glycemic Index: Low

CHICKEN WITH FIVE SPICES

Composition time: 10 minutes

Complete time: 30 minutes

Difficulty Level: Easy

Serving: 2

Components used:

- 2 skinless, boneless chicken breast halves
- 2.84g powdered five-spice; 1/8 teaspoon finely ginger; 28.3g orange zest (30 ml); and 1.42g rice wine vinegar

Method to cook:

- In a pot, add the vinegar, ginger, zest, juice, and five-spice powder. Pour over the chicken breasts in an 8 × 8-inch oven tray (20 x 20 cm).

- Turn the cook stove's temperature up to 350 degrees (180 degrees Celsius, or gas mark 4) Bake the tray covered for 40–45 minutes.
- Serve quickly over rice, with the juices poured over each plate.

Nutrients facts: 292 calories, 13 g fatty acid, 16 g starch, 24 g Amino acid

Glycemic Index: Low

CHICKEN WITH DRIED BEEF

Composition time: 10 minutes

Complete time: 45 minutes

Difficulty Level: Easy

Serving: 2

Components used:

- 43g canned coconut milk
- 4.2g freshly crushed ground pepper
- 6 big boneless, skinless chicken breasts
- 12 pieces bacon
- 1 21gs bone broth 1 (8-ounce) bottle dairy-free cream cheese
- 1 celery stalk

Method to cook:

- Rewarm the cook stove to 375 degrees Fahrenheit.
- Wrap 2 pieces of dry beef around each piece of chicken, then 1 slice of bacon. In a oven tray, arrange the wrapped chicken pieces.
- Add the broth, cream cheese, celery, coconut milk, and pepper in a pot. Over the chicken pieces, sprinkle batter.
- Bake for 1 hour, uncovered, in a rewarmed cook stove, or till chicken is cooked through.

Nutrients facts: 294 calories, 13 g fatty acid, 16 g starch, 24 g Amino acid

Glycemic Index: Low

TEQUILA CHICKEN

Composition time: 10 minutes

Complete time: 10 minutes

Difficulty Level: Easy

Serving: 2

Components used:

- 1 mug (235 ml) 9oz low-sodium chicken broth
- 3 garlic cloves, minced
- 2 chicken breasts, boneless and skinless
- a half-cup (120 ml) tequila
- a quarter cup (120 ml) juice of lime
- a pinch of cayenne
- 4.2g cayenne pepper
- 4.2g cumin powder
- a half teaspoon of coriander
- 15g (15 ml) extra virgin olive oil

Method to cook:

- Cook till the chicken breasts are soft in the liquid. Take off and cut into cubes. Set away, keeping the broth aside.
- Garlic should be cooked in olive oil. Stew, covered, for 1/2 hour after adding the fresh tomatoes (breaking them up). Reflame the chicken after adding it. Include the saved broth if the sauce gets too thick.

Nutrients facts: 218 calories, 13 g fatty acid, 16 g starch, 24 g Amino acid

Glycemic Index: Low

CHICKEN CURRY WITH ASPARAGUS

Composition time: 10 minutes

Complete time: 30 minutes

Difficulty Level: Easy

Serving: 2

Components used:

- 15g coconut oil
- 43g chopped onions
- 1 cinnamon
- 8.4g ground fenugreek
- 8.4g dry mustard
- 4.2g ground cumin
- 2 boneless, skinless chicken thighs, cut into 12-inch pieces
- Fine sea salt and ground ground pepper 1-pound asparagus, trimmed and cut into 2-inch pieces
- 1 (1312-ounce) can full-fat coconut milk
- Lime wcorners for dishing, garnished with fresh cilantro leaves

Method to cook:

- Warm the oil in a cast-iron pan over a moderate flame. The onions, cinnamon, fenugreek, dry mustard, and cumin should all be added at this point and prepareed for 4 minutes, or till the onions are soft.
- While you wait, soak off the chicken and thoroughly season both sides with some salt. Cook the chicken in a frying pan for 5 minutes on each side, or till it is golden brown and no longer pink inside.
- In a pot, add the asparagus, coconut milk, broth, stevia, turmeric, curry paste, and lime juice. Stir everything thoroughly to mix. Bring to a seethe, then reduce the flame to a seethe, cover, and prepare the asparagus for 5 minutes, or till it's cooked to your liking.

Nutrients facts: 292 calories, 13 g fatty acid, 16 g starch, 24 g Amino acid, Glycemic Index: Low

CHICKEN WITH APRICOTS & BOURBON

Composition time: 10 minutes

Complete time: 30 minutes

Difficulty Level: Moderate

Serving: 2

Components used:

- 900 g chicken breasts, boneless and skinless
- 28.3g butter
- 43g (55 g) pecans
- A quarter cup (80 g) apricot
- A quarter cup (60 ml) bourbon
- A quarter-cup (31 g) simple tomato sauce
- 28.3g mustard (spicy brown or Dijon)
- 1 smashed garlic clove or 2.84g minced garlic
- 21g (40 g) onion, minced
- 2 finely sliced scallions

Method to cook:

- Warm the cook stove to 176°C. In a big, heavy pan over moderate flame, brown them in 8.4g (28 g) butter.
- In a small, heavy pan, soften the leftover tablespoon (14 g) of butter and mix in the pecans while the breasts are browning. Stir them for some time over moderate flame, till they become brown. Turn off the flame

(and take off the tray from the burner if you're using an electric stove to avoid burning) and set aside.

- Add the preserves, bourbon, tomato sauce, mustard, garlic, and onion in a pot.
- Pour this batter into the tray when the chicken is light brown on both sides. To cover all sides of the chicken with the sauce, turn it over once or twice.

Nutrients facts: 299 calories, 13 g fatty acid, 15 g starch, 21 g Amino acid

Glycemic Index: Low

CHICKEN JERK ROTISSERIE

Composition time: 10 minutes

Complete time: 2 hours

Difficulty Level: Moderate

Serving: 2

Components used:

- a half-cup (80 g) onion
- 1 chicken to roast
- paprika, 4.2g
- g garlic powder (28.3g)
- 41g. jerk seasoning (12 g)

Method to cook:

- To get extremely small dice, pulse the onion in a food processor or mixer. Rub it all over the chicken, including the skin.
- In a pot, add the jerk spice, garlic powder, and paprika.
- Allow the chicken to marinade for upto 2 hours after applying the rub all over it. Roast for 1 to 2 hours at 176°C (180°C, gas mark 4) in the cook stove.

Nutrients facts: 318 calories, 13 g fatty acid, 16 g starch, 24 g Amino acid

Glycemic Index: Low

CITRUS CHICKEN

Composition time: 10 minutes

Complete time: 10 minutes

Difficulty Level: Easy

Serving: 2

Components used:

- 1 a half pound (680 g) chicken breasts, boneless and skinless

- a quarter cup (60 ml) extra virgin olive oil
- a half-cup (120 ml) juice of lime
- a quarter cup (60 ml) juice of a lemon
- 4.2g flakes of red pepper
- 4.2g (2 g) chopped garlic
- 15g (8 g) (3 g) ginger root, grated
- a quarter cup (6 g) Splenda
- 4 thinly sliced scallions
- 28g. (2 g) cilantro

Method to cook:

- If required, slice the chicken into 4 portions. With a slanted lid, cook the chicken in the olive oil over moderate flame.
- Add the lime juice, lemon juice, red pepper flakes, garlic, gingerroot, and Splenda while it's cooking.
- Sprinkle lime juice batter into the tray after the chicken has become brown on both sides (approximately 4 to 5 minutes each side), and flip the breasts over to coat all sides.
- Cook for a further 2 to 3 minutes on each side, then move the chicken to serving dishes, scraping the tray liquid over the chicken.

Nutrients facts: 298 calories, 13 g fatty acid, 16 g starch, 24 g Amino acid

Glycemic Index: Low

LIME CHICKEN FAJITAS

Composition time: 10 minutes

Complete time: 30 minutes

Difficulty Level: Moderate

Serving: 2

Components used:

- flank steak or chicken breast, 1 pound (455 g)
- a half-cup (120 ml) juice of lime
- a quarter cup (4 g) cilantro
- a quarter cup (60 ml) vinegar (white)
- a quarter cup (60 ml) extra virgin olive oil
- 3 teaspoons of oil (45 ml) vinegar balsamic
- cayenne pepper, 15g (5 g)
- 3 garlic cloves, minced
- 15g of oil (6 g) peppercorns

Method to cook:

- In a large mixing basin, combine all the ingredients except from the meat. Marinate the meat in the marinade for the entire night. Set the grill to high flame.
- Take off the marinade and bring to a seethe in a cast iron pan. Take off from the cook stove and set aside to chill. Grill the meat, basting it with the marinade till it's done. Make long, thin strips out of it.

Nutrients facts: 363 calories, 13 g fatty acid, 16 g starch, 24 g Amino acid

Glycemic Index: Low

CHICKEN LEGS BRAISED IN CURRY

Composition time: 10 minutes

Complete time: 60 minutes

Difficulty Level: Easy

Serving: 2

Components used:

- 21g avocado or coconut oil
- 21g diced onions
- 15g peeled and grated fresh ginger
- 15g minced garlic
- 85g sliced button mushrooms
- chicken legs
- 4.2g fine sea salt
- 85g homemade or store-bought chicken bone broth
- 43g full-fat coconut milk
- 28.3g red curry paste
- 28.3g lime juice scallions

Method to cook:

- Warm the oil in a large cast-iron pan over moderate flame. The onions should be cooked for 2 minutes, or till soft. Include the ginger and garlic and continue preparing for extra minute. Cook the mushrooms for 2 minutes, or till golden brown, after adding them.
- On both sides, season the chicken with salt. Put the chicken in the tray and sear for about two minutes on each side, or till golden brown. In a pot, add the broth, coconut milk, and curry paste. Cook the chicken for 30 to 40 minutes with the lid on, mixing continuously to deglaze the tray's bottom, till it is well flameed through

- Include the lime juice and mix well.

Nutrients facts: 317 calories, 13 g fatty acid, 16 g starch, 24 g Amino acid

Glycemic Index: Low

MEXICAN CHICKEN & RICE

Composition time: 10 minutes

Complete time: 10 minutes

Difficulty Level: Easy

Serving: 2

Components used:

- (225 g) tomato sauce
- 4.2g cumin powder
- a quarter teaspoon of onion powder
- 1/8 teaspoon powdered garlic
- a quarter teaspoon of cocoa
- 15g chili powder (7.5 g)
- 2 cooked and sliced boneless skinless chicken breasts
- 85g rice (195 g)
- 85g shredded cheddar cheese (115 g)

Method to cook:

- In a small pot, mix 2/3 of the fresh tomato sauce with the seasonings. Cooked chicken should be added now.
- Put the sauce on a low flame setting and whisk it periodically.
- Make the rice. When the rice is done, whisk in the leftover 1/3 of the fresh tomato sauce.

Nutrients facts: 326 calories, 13 g fatty acid, 16 g starch, 24 g Amino acid

Glycemic Index: Low

BBQ CHICKEN BREASTS

Composition time: 10 minutes

Complete time: 30 minutes

Difficulty Level: Moderate

Serving: 2

Components used:

- 43g Simple BBQ Sauce
- 4 skinless, boneless breast halves of chicken
- 3 firm and slightly ripe avocados

- 1 (1-pound) package thin-cut bacon (about 20 strips)

Method to cook:

- Bring the cook stove back up to 425 degrees. A rimmed baking sheet should be lined with baking paper.
- Chicken strips should be covered in BBQ sauce.
- After the avocados have been peeled and pitted, chop them into thick fry shapes.

Each slice of bread should have a piece of bacon wrapped around it.

- Put the chicken and bacon-wrapped avocado pieces on the baking sheet. Bake for 20 to 25 minutes, or till the chicken liquid runs clear and the avocados are soft.

Nutrients facts: 299 calories, 13 g fatty acid, 15 g starch, 21 g Amino acid

Glycemic Index: Low

FRYING PAN CASSEROLE WITH GROUND BEEF

Composition time: 5 minutes

Complete time: 45-60 minutes

Difficulty Level: Easy

Serving: 2

Components used:

- 1 pound of extra-lean beef (90 percent lean) beef
- 4 oz. rotini (multigrain or whole grain)
- 1 (14.5-ounce) may no longer be used
- stirred tomatoes with salt
- 143gs green bell pepper
- 4 oz. mushrooms, sliced
- Ketchup, 21g
- Worcestershire sauce, 15g
- 15g. balsamic vinaigrette
- 85g of water
- Salt (1.42g)

Method to cook:

- In a large nonstick frying pan, Warm the flame to moderate. For three minutes, toss the meat often while cooking it in batches. Trim the meat of any extra fat.
- In a pot, add the leftover ingredients. To cook the noodles, bring the brew to a seethe, then Reduce the flame, cover it, and finely cook for 15 minutes.

Nutrients facts: 292 calories, 13 g fatty acid, 16 g starch, 24 g Amino acid

Glycemic Index: Low

BEEF BURRITOS

Composition time: 10 minutes

Complete time: 30 minutes

Difficulty Level: Easy

Serving: 2

Components used:

- 1.5 pound beef chuck pot roast
- 28.3g taco sauce Verde
- 8.4g minced garlic
- 1 scallions or spring onions, big

- 2 chopped jalapeño peppers
- 4.2g cayenne pepper
- 1/4 tsp. cumin and 14 tsp. salt

Method to cook:

- Trim away as much fat as possible from the meat.
- Combine all ingredients in a slow cooker and cover with the lid.
- Cook for 8 hours or till the meat is very soft.
- Move the beef to a chopping board and shred it with two forks (one to hold the meat and the other to shred it.)
- In a serving dish, put the shredded meat.
- Pour 43g of the cooking liquid into the pot and thoroughly combine.

Nutrients facts: 272 calories, 13 g fatty acid, 16 g starch, 24 g Amino acid

Glycemic Index: Low

BEEF LIVER BURGERS

Composition time: 10 minutes

Complete time: 30 minutes

Difficulty Level: Easy

Serving: 2

Components used:

- 1 pound of beef or bison into tiny pieces
- 8oz beef liver, cut into small pieces
- 37g stevia-free ketchup
- 3 teaspoons garlic salt, split

Method to cook:

- Add the ground beef, liver, ketchup, and 28.3g garlic salt in a pot. From 4 to 6 burger patties from the brew.
- Over moderate flame, warm the oil in a cast iron frying pan. On top of the burgers, include the final teaspoon of garlic salt. Cook till well done, about 8 to 10 minutes per side.

Nutrients facts: 264 calories, 13 g fatty acid, 16 g starch, 24 g Amino acid

Glycemic Index: Low

BEEF WITH SESAME SAUCE

Composition time: 10 minutes

Complete time: 40 minutes

Difficulty Level: Easy

Serving: 2

Components used:

- a quarter-cup (30 ml) extra virgin olive oil
- a quarter-cup (26 g) stevia
- a quarter-cup (30 ml) Soy Sauce
- 2 garlic cloves garlic
- a quarter cup (25 g) green onions
- to taste ground pepper
- 1 pound (455 g) cut-in-strips round steak
- 15g (8 g) roasted sesame seeds

Method to cook:

- Mix 15g (15 ml) oil, stevia, soy sauce, garlic, green onions, and pepper in a pot. Marinate the meat for upto 30 minutes in this marinade.
- In a frying pan or wok, flame the leftover oil. Stir-fry the meat with the marinade. Serve with rice and sesame seeds on top.

Nutrients facts: 239 calories, 13 g fatty acid, 16 g starch, 24 g Amino acid

Glycemic Index: Low

SWEET SOY FLANK

Composition time: 10 minutes

Complete time: 45 minutes

Difficulty Level: Easy

Serving: 2

Components used:

- 21g soy sauce (mild)
- Ketchup, 28.3g
- 15g. balsamic vinaigrette
- A quarter teaspoon of garlic powder
- 2.84g powdered onion
- 1.42g pepper flakes (dry)
- Flank steak, 1 1/2 pound
- 28.3g green onion, finely chopped (optional)

Method to cook:

- In a gallon-size plastic bag, mix all ingredients (excluding green onion), close

firmly, and flip back and forth till thoroughly mixed. Refrigerate for upto 8 hours and up to 48 hours.

- Warm the grill pan to moderate. Spray the grill pan with nonstick spray oil.
- Take the steak out of the marinade and throw it away. In order to dry the steak, use paper towels. Cook for four minutes on each side. (Note: if you continue to boil it, it will turn tough.) Put the meat on a chopping board and let it aside for 10 minutes before cutting thinly across the grain.

Nutrients facts: 350 calories, 13 g fatty acid, 16 g starch, 24 g Amino acid

Glycemic Index: Low

BEEF WITH RICE NOODLES

Composition time: 10 minutes

Complete time: 40 minutes

Difficulty Level: Moderate

Serving: 2

Components used:

- Boneless beef round steak, 13/4 pound (795 g)
- 4 tablespoons sake or sherry (60 ml) split
- 15g of oil (6 g) ginger root, finely chopped
- 37g vegetable oil (45 ml), divided
- 4oz (115 g) rice noodles 1 garlic clove, smashed
- 400g thinly sliced bok Choy
- thinly sliced green olives

Method to cook:

- Trim any excess fat from the beef steak. Slice the meat into 1/4-inch (5 mm) strips diagonally. In a medium glass or plastic dish, mix the meat, 28.3 (30 ml) sake, gingerroot, 8.4g (10 ml) oil, and garlic.
- 30 minutes after covering, place in the fridge. Rice noodles should be placed in a large mixing basin. Boiling water should be placed halfway up the container. Ten minutes of waiting should be given before full draining. Chop the veggies roughly.
- Flame one teaspoon of oil in a wok. The meat batter should be stirred for about 5 minutes or till the beef is well cooked.
- In a pot, add the rice noodles, bok Choy, and onions. Cook the Bok Choy for 4 minutes or till it is crisp-very soft.

Nutrients facts: 292 calories, 13 g fatty acid, 16 g starch, 24 g Amino acid

Glycemic Index: Low

QUICHE TACOS

Composition time: 10 minutes

Complete time: 45-60 minutes

Difficulty Level: Easy

Serving: 2

Components used:

- extra-lean ground beef
- 28g. taco seasoning (8 g)
- water, 43g (120 ml)
- 43g (58 g) low-fat shredded cheese
- 2oz (55 g) chopped green chilies, seeded
- three eggs
- 85g fat-free evaporated milk (235 mL)

Method to cook:

- Warm the cook stove to 375 degrees Fahrenheit (190 degrees Celsius). In a frying pan, brown the meat. Drain. Sprinkle taco seasoning mix and water, then cover and prepare for 15 minutes. Allow 10 minutes for chilling.
- Mix in the cheese and chilies well. Fill a pie pan with the brew after spraying it with nonstick vegetable oil spray.
- Mix eggs and milk in a pot. Mix till completely smooth. Bake for 40 to 45 minutes, or till custard is set, in a Warmed cook stove.
- Allow 5 minutes for the pie to rest before eating.

Nutrients facts: 262 calories, 13 g fatty acid, 16 g starch, 24 g Amino acid

Glycemic Index: Low

GROUND BEEF AND CABBAGE SLAW

Composition time: 10 minutes

Complete time: 30 minutes

Difficulty Level: Easy

Serving: 2

Components used:

- 1 pound ground beef
- 1 (16-ounce) bag cabbage slaw mix
- 37g coconut aminos

- 15g fish sauce

Method to cook:

- Olive oil should be flamed at a moderate temperature in a big pan. Cook for about 7 minutes, continuously rotating the meat, till the meat is browned. Cook for about 15 minutes, regularly tossing the cabbage till it has wilted.
- Cook for a further five minutes after adding the coconut aminos and fish sauce.

Nutrients facts: 299 calories, 13 g fatty acid, 15 g starch, 21 g Amino acid

Glycemic Index: Low

EASY-TO-MAKE MEATLOAF

Composition time: 10 minutes

Complete time: 15 minutes

Difficulty Level: Easy

Serving: 2

Components used:

- 12 oz. extra-lean beef (90 percent lean) beef in the ground
- 43g oats (quick-cooking)
- 1 (14-ounce) container thawed frozen pepper stir-fry
- A quarter cup of egg repayment
- 4.2g oregano leaves, dried
- Pizza sauce (about 6oz)
- 15g. Parmesan cheese, grated (optional)

Method to cook:

- Warm the cook stove to 350 degrees Fahrenheit. In a medium mixing basin, include the meat, oats, stir fry, egg, Worcestershire sauce, oregano, and all but 21g of the pizza sauce and mix well. Put the brew in a nonstick loaf pan that has been sprayed with spray oil.
- Bake for 1 hour or till an internal temperature of 160°F is reached when a meat thermometer is used. Spread the leftover pizza sauce equally over the top and garnish with cheese (if preferred). Set aside for 5 minutes before cutting into 8 pieces.

Nutrients facts: 292 calories, 13 g fatty acid, 16 g starch, 24 g Amino acid

Glycemic Index: Low

BLEU PATTY BURGER

Composition time: 10 minutes

Complete time: 10 minutes

Difficulty Level: Easy

Serving: 2

Components used:

- Burger patty Bleu Burger, pound (150 g)
- g blue cheese crumbles
- 15g. sweet red onion (finely chopped)

Method to cook:

- Using your favorite technique, cook the burger. Top with the bleu cheese and let it soften when it's nearly done to your preference.
- Take off the tray from the flame, place it on a pot, and garnish with the onion.

Nutrients facts: 248 calories, 13 g fatty acid, 16 g starch, 24 g Amino acid

Glycemic Index: Moderate

CINNAMON ROASTED VEAL

Composition time: 10 minutes

Complete time: 45-60 minutes

Difficulty Level: Easy

Serving: 2

Components used:

- 1 kilogram veal roast (bottom shell)
- A pinch of some salt
- 28.3g brandy
- shallots
- Soup greens (12 bunch)
- 28.3g of oil
- garlic cloves
- 1 stick of cinnamon
- ground peppercorns
- 500 milliliters of milk
- 41g. sauce thickener (mild)

Method to cook:

- Clean the meat by rinsing it and patting it dry. Season with salt, pepper, and a dash of brandy. Onions are peeled and chopped. Soup greens should be washed and chopped finely.

- Fry the meat in a pan with oil. Fry the onions and soup greens for some time. Add the cloves, cinnamon, peppercorns, and milk to a pot.
- After that, cover and prepare for around 12 hours. Take off the roast, drain the sauce, and season to taste with some salt. Open the roast and serve it with the sauce.

Nutrients facts: 367 calories, 13 g fatty acid, 16 g starch, 24 g Amino acid

Glycemic Index: Low

CHINESE BEEF & BROCCOLI WITH SOUP

Composition time: 10 minutes

Complete time: 45 minutes

Difficulty Level: Easy

Serving: 2

Components used:

- 2 pounds cubed beef stew meat
- 15g tamari, or 21g coconut aminos
- 28.3g plus 8.4g coconut oil, divided
- 85g chopped onions
- 5 garlic cloves, minced
- 15g peeled and grated fresh ginger (optional)
- 48oz broccoli florets into bite-sized pieces
- 48oz beef bone broth
- 8.4g fish sauce

Method to cook:

- Cut any stew meat portions that are bigger than 1 inch into smaller pieces. In a medium-sized dish, put the meat.
- Flip in the tamari to coat. Place in the refrigerator for upto 1 hour or overnight to marinate.
- In a large cast iron pan or Dutch cook stove, soften 15g coconut oil over moderate Warm. Add half of the steak when the oil is smoking hot.
- Spread the meat evenly throughout the cast iron pan and finely cook for 1 minute without mixing. Stir or flip the meat with tongs, then spread it out throughout the cast iron pan and prepare for another minute. Make sure the meat isn't overcooked; it should be just cooked through but still quite soft. Move the meat to a lidded dish.
- Empty the cast iron pan of any surplus liquid. Rep Step 2 with the leftover meat

and another spoonful of coconut oil. Wrap the tray snugly with the lid and include the second batch of cooked meat and any liquids from the cast iron pan.

- Include the leftover 28.3g coconut oil in the Warming pot, along with the onions, garlic, and ginger, if using. Flip the onions in the oil to coat them, season with some salt, and fry for approximately 5 minutes, turning periodically till soft.
- Sprinkle broccoli and beef broth, then Lowerto low Warm. Taste after adding the fish sauce and sweetness; if needed, add additional salt or sweetener.
- Cook for 4 minutes or till the broccoli is very soft.

Nutrients facts: 327 calories, 13 g fatty acid, 16 g starch, 24 g Amino acid Glycemic Index: Low

CRUNCHY PEKING BURGERS

Composition time: 10 minutes

Complete time: 50 minutes

Difficulty Level: Easy

Serving: 2

Components used:

- 455 g beef patty
- Drained (100 g) canned water chestnuts
- green onions
- 14 oz. (60 ml) tamari
- Splenda, 4.2g
- garlic cloves, smashed
- 4.2g minced garlic
- 128g. ginger (grated)
- 1 table salt
- 1/4 tsp. ginger (grated)

Method to cook:

- A tabletop electric grill should be Warmed. Cutting the scallions and chopping the fresh water chestnuts. Add them with the rest of the burger ingredients in a pot and thoroughly combine them with clean hands. Make four burgers and prepare them. 5 minutes of cooking.
- Add the preserves, soy sauce, and ginger to a pot while the burgers are cooking.

Nutrients facts: 293 calories, 13 g fatty acid, 16 g starch, 24 g Amino acid

Glycemic Index: Low

BEEF SALSA VERDE

Composition time: 10 minutes

Complete time: 45-60 minutes

Difficulty Level: Easy

Serving: 2

Components used:

- 1 sliced tomato,
- half cup parsley flowers
- half cup basil flowers
- 2 cloves of garlic
- 28.3g capers (drained)
- 1 fillet of anchovies, sliced into pieces
- 85g olive oil
- 28g juice of lime
- season with salt to taste
- 1–8.4g ground pepper
- 750g (about 25oz) thin sirloin/fillet steak

Method to cook:

- In a juicer or mixer, mix parsley, basil, garlic, capers, tomato, and anchovy fillet; gradually sprinkle in olive oil till mixed. Mix in the lime juice, some salt till smooth and thoroughly mixed. Season with Salt, then put aside.
- Season the meat and grill or pan-fried it to your liking.
- When the meat is done, thinly slice it and sprinkle it with salsa Verde.

Nutrients facts: 314 calories, 13 g fatty acid, 16 g starch, 24 g Amino acid

Glycemic Index: Low

CHIPOTLE BURGERS

Composition time: 10 minutes

Complete time: 10 minutes

Difficulty Level: Moderate

Serving: 2

Components used:

- Two kilos (910 g) beef patty
- 43g chipotle chilies
- 21g 2 smashed garlic cloves (40 g) onion, grated
- 1/28g. sodium
- A 6 oz. (170 g) Monterey slices of Jack cheese

Method to cook:

- Put everything in a huge mixing basin, except the cheese, and squish it all together with clean hands till everything is thoroughly combined. 6 inch (2.5 cm) thick burgers Place your burgers on a platter and refrigerate for upto an hour before grilling.
- Start your fire—you'll need a well-ashed charcoal or a gas grill set to medium or lower. Grill the burgers for 7 to 10 minutes on each side or till juices flow clear, using a water bottle to control flare-ups.

Nutrients facts: 292 calories, 13 g fatty acid, 16 g starch, 24 g Amino acid

Glycemic Index: Low

CHILI BEEF SAUSAGE

Composition time: 10 minutes

Complete time: 25 minutes

Difficulty Level: Moderate

Serving: 2

Components used:

- Breakfast sausage, 1 pound
- One pound (455 g) ground beef that is particularly lean
- 4 mugs (1 kg) kidney beans, without salt, boiled or canned
- 1 mug (150 g) green bell pepper
- 1 mug (100 g) celery, sliced
- tomato paste with no salt added
- 2.84g garlic, minced
- Chili powder (about 28.3g)

Method to cook:

- Cook sausage and ground beef in a pan over moderate-high flame till browned; drain excess oil. Put the meat in the slow cooker.
- Mix the leftover ingredients in a pot. Cook on low for 8 to 10 hours, covered.

Nutrients facts: 257 calories, 13 g fatty acid, 16 g starch, 24 g Amino acid

Glycemic Index: Low

ORANGE STEAK

Composition time: 10 minutes

Complete time: 55 minutes

Difficulty Level: Easy

Serving: 2

Components used:

- 15g. orange juice (45 ml)
- 15g dry sherry (15 ml)
- a tablespoon of soy sauce
- 15g. Splenda (stevia substitute)
- 12 to 16oz (340 to 455 g) steak, 1/2 inch (1.3 cm) thick—rib eye, sirloin, strip steaks

Method to cook:

- Mix the orange juice, sherry, soy sauce, Splenda, and garlic in a pot. Put the steak on a platter and sprinkle orange juice batter over it, turning it over a few times to evenly Wrap the top.
- Allow 2 to 3 minutes for the steak to rest.
- Broil the steak as near to a hot flame as possible till it's done to your liking—for me, 4 1/2 to 5 minutes on each side is about perfect.

Nutrients facts: 279 calories, 13 g fatty acid, 16 g starch, 24 g Amino acid

Glycemic Index: Moderate

VEAL ROLLS WITH TUNA SAUCE

Composition time: 10 minutes

Complete time: 20 minutes

Difficulty Level: Easy

Serving: 2

Components used:

- 2 cans oil-packed tuna fillets (185 g each)
- Crème fraiche, 28g.
- 15g. lemon extract
- 1/2 bunch parsley (flat-leaf)
- 28.3g capers
- Seasoning with some salt
- 2 peeled and hard-boiled eggs
- veal legs, thinly sliced (approx. 80 g each)
- 2 onions, peeled
- 500 g tomatoes, chunky
- A handful of thyme leaves
- 1 to 28.3g balsamic vinegar

Method to cook:

- Take off the tuna from the can and set aside 37g of the oil. In a juicer or mixer, puree half of the tuna, crème fraiche, and lemon juice.

- Wash the parsley, coarsely cut it, and stir it into the tuna puree with the capers and 4.2g caper stock. Season with Salt. Eggs should be quartered.
- Season the schnitzel with some salt, then spread the tuna cream on one side and garnish with the egg quarters. Roll the meat into a cylinder and secure it with a toothpick.
- Peel the onions and chop them into thin rings. In a roaster, flame the tuna oil. Fry the roulades, then take them off and cook the onions in the frying oil for some time.
- Include the fresh tomatoes, thyme, and roulades, and bring to a seethe for some time. Cover and prepare for approximately 30 minutes at 200 degrees (convection: 180 degrees) in a Warmed cook stove. 6. Take off the roulades from the tray. Flame the leftover tuna in the sauce for some time. Vinegar, some salt to taste.

Nutrients facts: 229 calories, 13 g fatty acid, 16 g starch, 24 g Amino acid

Glycemic Index: Moderate

PEPPERONCINI BEEF

Composition time: 10 minutes

Complete time: 50 minutes

Difficulty Level: Easy

Serving: 2

Components used:

- to 3 pounds (0.9 to 1.3 kg) chuck roast (boneless) in a pot
- 85g (225 g) pepperoncini peppers, including the vinegar
- Guar or xanthan gum,
- 1/2 medium onion, diced

Method to cook:

- Put the meat in the slow cooker, cover it with the pepperoncini, and scatter the onions on top. Put the cover on the slow cooker and set it to Low for 8 hours.
- When it's done, take off the meat and place it on a pot, then take off the peppers using a slotted spoon and lay them on top of the roast. Thick the fluids in the cast iron pan with guar or xanthan gum, season with some salt, and serve with the roast.

Nutrients facts: 292 calories, 13 g fatty acid, 16 g starch, 24 g Amino acid

Glycemic Index: Low

FIREHOUSE BEEF

Composition time: 10 minutes

Complete time: 30 minutes

Difficulty Level: Easy

Serving: 2

Components used:

- Two kilos (910 g) chuckling
- 43gs of coffee
- onion, peeled
- 4 garlic cloves (minced)
- A third cup (23 g) powdered red chili
- Paprika, 41g.
- 4 tsp. cumin powder
- Ketchup (non-stevia)
- A quarter cup (33 g) pureed tomatoes
- 1 can (410 g/1.12 oz.)
- Tomatoes
- 360 ml beer
- Splenda, 4.2g
- Salt (2128g.)
- Black soybeans

Method to cook:

- Brown the meat over a moderate flame in a large, heavy-frying pan. Put it in a slow cooker after draining it.
- The leftover components should be added now. Toss it all around. Cook for 8 hours on low in a covered slow cooker.

Nutrients facts: 327 calories, 13 g fatty acid, 16 g starch, 24 g Amino acid

Glycemic Index: Low

BRAISED BEEF IN RED WINE SAUCE

Composition time: 10 minutes

Complete time: 45 minutes

Difficulty Level: Easy

Serving: 2

Components used:

- 200 g carrots (about)
- Celeriac, 200 g

- Rosemary, 2 sprigs
- 3 thyme stalks
- 1 kilogram of beef from the thigh
- Onions, 200 g
- Three garlic cloves
- 500 ml beef broth 375 ml red wine
- 15g of tomato paste
- 1-2 garlic cloves
- 1 bay leaf honeydew, grated
- Polenta (250 g) (corn grits)

Method to cook:

- Slice the carrots into slices and dice the celery. Tomatoes should be scalded, then quenched, peeled, and diced. Herbs should be chopped.
- Season the meat with some salt before frying it. Toast the celery, carrots, shallots, and garlic for some time. Red wine and stock are used to deglaze the tray. Tomato paste, tomatoes, cloves, rosemary, thyme, and bay leaves are added to the pot.
- Cover and prepare for about 2 hours on low flame. In between turns, rotate the roast. Bring the milk, salt, pepper, and honeydew to a seethe for the polenta. Mix in the semolina.
- Soak for approximately 10 minutes on the switched-off burner. Stir everything together at the same time. Keep the roast flamed in the cook stove.

Nutrients facts: 292 calories, 13 g fatty acid, 16 g starch, 24 g Amino acid

Glycemic Index: Low

SMOKEY SLOPPY JOES

Composition time: 10 minutes

Complete time: 20 minutes

Difficulty Level: Easy

Serving: 2

Components used:

- 15g. canola seed oil
- 1 pound extra-lean ground beef (90 percent lean)
- 85g onions, diced
- 85g green bell pepper
- 1 can (14.5 oz.) stewed tomatoes with no salt added
- 4.2g of stevia
- 15g. paprika (smoked)

- Worcestershire sauce, 15g
- 15g. apple cider vinegar
- 1.42g allspice powder
- A half teaspoon of salt
- 4.2g cayenne pepper
- hamburger buns (whole)

Method to cook:

- In a big frying pan, flame the oil over moderate flame. Brown the meat, mixing every now and again. Take off any excess fat from the steak and mix with the other ingredients (excluding the buns). Bring to a seethe over moderate flame, then lower to low flame, cover, and finely cook for 15 minutes, or till veggies are soft.
- Take off the cover and prepare over moderate flame to come to a seethe. Boil for 3–4 minutes, or till the sauce has thickened somewhat. Mix all ingredients in a big dish and serve with hamburger buns.

Nutrients facts: 292 calories, 13 g fatty acid, 16 g starch, 24 g Amino acid, Glycemic Index: Low

CHIPOTLE MEATLOAVES

Composition time: 10 minutes

Complete time: 30 minutes

Difficulty Level: Moderate

Serving: 2

Components used:

- 1 pound beef (ground)
- 21g bread crumbs (soft whole)
- 1 big, gently beaten egg
- teaspoons water 4 tablespoons cilantro
- 2.84g salt 4.2g chipotle chili powder, divided
- 1 tomato sauce can (15oz)
- Fresh cilantro (optional)

Method to cook:

- In a pot, add ground beef, bread crumbs, egg, 28.3g cilantro, 2.84g chipotle chili powder, and 2.84g salt. Form the meatballs into 24 one-inch balls. Warm a large nonstick frying pan over a moderate flame. Cook for 8 minutes or till meatballs is browned on both sides in a pan.
- Bring to a seethe with the leftover 28.3g cilantro and the leftover 2.84g chipotle chili spice. Lower flame to low, cover, and

prepare for 8 to 10 minutes, mixing continuously.

- Serve meatballs on skewers or toothpicks on a plate. If desired, garnish with cilantro.

Nutrients facts: 294 calories, 13 g fatty acid, 16 g starch, 24 g Amino acid

Glycemic Index: Low

FRENCH MEATLOAF

Composition time: 10 minutes

Complete time: 20 minutes

Difficulty Level: Easy

Serving: 2

Components used:

- Corn in a can (drained weight 300 g)
- shallots
- Two garlic cloves
- 1 each of red, yellow, and green bell peppers
- 1 chili pepper, red
- 1 bunch parsley (flat-leaf)
- Margarine (40 g)
- A pinch of some salt
- 1 pound of beef mince
- Breadcrumbs, 4 tbsp.
- Three eggs
- tablespoons mustard

Method to cook:

- Prepare the corn by draining it through a sieve. Onions and garlic should be diced.
- The peppers and chili should be soaked and diced. Parsley should be washed and roughly chopped. In a large pan, soften the margarine. Fry the onions, garlic, paprika and chili for about 5 minutes.
- Take off from flame, season with some salt, and set aside to chill. Knead the minced meat, breadcrumbs, eggs and mustard and season with some salt. Mix in the vegetables and parsley and pour everything into an oiled loaf pan.
- Bake in a Warmed cook stove at 200 degrees for about 45 minutes. Sprinkle with herbs if desired before eating.

Nutrients facts: 292 calories, 13 g fatty acid, 16 g starch, 24 g Amino acid

Glycemic Index: Low

ROASTED PEPPER SIRLOIN

Composition time: 10 minutes

Complete time: 20 minutes

Difficulty Level: Easy

Serving: 2

Components used:

- 1 pound of meat Petite Roast of Top Sirloin (1 1/2 to 2 pounds)
- 15g pepper, seasoned
- 43g blue cheese crumbles
- 21g softened butter
- 15g green onion
- 12 fluidoz 1 red onion, sliced into 1/2-inch thick slices and split into rings Broccolini, trimmed and 85g of water

Method to cook:

- Warm the cook stove to 325 degrees Fahrenheit. Apply seasoned pepper to the whole surface of the meat roast.
- In a small roasting pan, put the roast fat-side up on a rack. Put the point of a cook stoveproof meat thermometer in the thickest portion of the steak. Cover, but do not add water. Roast for 60-75 minutes at 325°F for medium rare to medium doneness. In the meantime, add the cheese, butter, and green onion to a pot; set aside.
- Spray a large nonstick frying pan with nonstick spray oil, then include the broccolini, onion, and water. Over moderate flame, cook the covered dish for 3 minutes. Cook for a further two to four minutes after removing the cover. Take the tray off the stove. Include the blue cheese batter in 28.3g straight quickly.
- The roast should be taken off, set on a carving board, and covered with a sheet. Give yourself a 10-minute break.
- Slice the roast and sprinkle with salt to taste. Serve with the leftover vegetables and blue cheese butter.

Nutrients facts: 274 calories, 13 g fatty acid, 16 g starch, 24 g Amino acid

Glycemic Index: Low

ASIAN VEGETABLE SALAD

Composition time: 5 minutes

Complete time: 20 minutes

Difficulty Level: Easy

Serving: 2

Components used:

- 4 limes, 1 lime zest and 2 lime juice
- 21g rice syrup (brown)
- Soy sauce
- 28.3g rice vinegar (brown)
- 32oz Napa cabbage, finely chopped
- 1 seeded and julienned red bell pepper
- 1 bunch green onions
- 85g sprouted mung beans
- 43g cilantro
- 43g basil leaves
- 1 Serrano chili, thinly cut on the diagonal (take off the seeds for reduced flame)
- 8.4g mint

Method to cook:

- Mix the lime zest and juice, brown rice syrup, and soy sauce in a pot (if using).
- Flip together the brown rice vinegar, cabbage, pepper, green onion, sprouts, cilantro, basil, chili, and mint in a pot.
- Serve with Ponzu Sauce on the side.

Nutrients facts: 251 calories, 13 g fatty acid, 16 g starch, 24 g Amino acid

Glycemic Index: Low

LENTILS & FRESH HERB SALAD

Composition time: 5 minutes

Complete time: 20 minutes

Difficulty Level: Easy

Serving: 2

Components used:

- 43g washed green lentils
- 3 mugs vegetable broth or vegetable stock
- 1 lemon's zest and 2 lemons' juice
- 2 garlic cloves, peeled and minced
- 43g cilantro, finely chopped
- 8.4g mint, finely chopped
- arugula, 32oz

Method to cook:

- In a pan over a moderate flame, add the lentils and vegetable stock and bring to a

Boil. Raise to low flame, cover, and finely cook for 35 to 45 minutes or till lentils are cooked but not mushy.

- Put the lentils in a pot after draining them. Mix in the lemon zest and juice, as well as the garlic, cilantro, mint, green onion, and some salt.
- Divide the arugula among four different dishes to serve. Serve the lentil salad over the greens, topped with finely sliced green onion.

Nutrients facts: 361 calories, 13 g fatty acid, 16 g starch, 24 g Amino acid

Glycemic Index: Low

BERRIES SALAD

Composition time: 10 minutes

Complete time: 20 minutes

Difficulty Level: Easy

Serving: 2

Components used:

- 2 43g berries
- 21g apple cider vinegar plus 8.4g
- 21g rice syrup (brown)
- 43g minced green onion
- 2 celery stalks
- 8.4g tarragon, minced
- 1 cored and diced Bosc pear
- 43g dried cranberries, sweetened with fruit

Method to cook:

- 5 cups of water should be brought to a seethe in a medium cast iron pan before adding the berries. Over moderate flame, bring the brew back to a seethe. Then, Reduce the flame to medium, Wrap the pot, and stew it for 134 hours, or till the berries are soft. The berries should be taken out of the tray and chilled after being soaked.

- Combine all of the leftover ingredients in a pot. Well include the chilled berries. For one hour before eating, chill.

Nutrients facts: 217 calories, 13 g fatty acid, 16 g starch, 24 g Amino acid

Glycemic Index: Low

TOMATO, CUCUMBER AND MINT SALAD

Composition time: 10 minutes

Complete time: 20 minutes

Difficulty Level: Easy

Serving: 2

Components used:

- 21g balsamic vinegar
- 2 big tomatoes, diced
- 2 big cucumbers
- diced 2 green onions
- 28.3g mint, finely chopped

Method to cook:

- Add salt and freshly ground pepper to taste.
- Add the fresh tomatoes, cucumber, green onions, balsamic vinegar, and mint in a pot. Pepper some salt to taste. Allow 30 minutes to sit before eating.

Nutrients facts: 231 calories, 13 g fatty acid, 16 g starch, 24 g Amino acid

Glycemic Index: Low

GRAINS SALAD

Composition time: 0 minutes

Complete time: 10 minutes

Difficulty Level: Easy

Serving: 2

Components used:

- 400g brown basmati rice 2 limes, zest and juice
- 21g brown rice syrup 14 cup brown rice vinegar

- a cup of currants (12 cup)
- 1/2 tiny red onion, peeled and minced
- 6 green onions, coarsely chopped
- 1 minced jalapeno pepper
- curry powder (about 15g)
- 21g cilantro

Method to cook:

- Strain the rice after rinsing it in chill water. Mix it with 32oz of cold water in a cast iron pan. Bring to a seethe over a moderate flame, then lower to moderate flame and finely cook for 45 to 50 minutes, or till the rice is soft.
- While the rice is cooking, add the currants, green onion, red onion, jalapeño pepper, curry powder, cilantro, some salt in a pot with the lime zest and juice. Rice that has excess water take offd should be added to the pot and well mixed.

Nutrients facts: 189 calories, 13 g fatty acid, 16 g starch, 24 g Amino acid

Glycemic Index: Low

ARGULA & QUINOA SALAD

Composition time: 10 minutes

Complete time: 10 minutes

Difficulty Level: Easy

Serving: 2

Components used:

- 43g quinoa 2 oranges' zest and juice
- 1 lime's zest and juice
- 21g rice vinegar (brown)
- arugula, 32oz
- 1 small peeled and thinly sliced red onion
- 1 seeded red bell pepper, cut into 12-inch small pieces
- teaspoons toasted pine nuts

Method to cook:

- Drain the quinoa after rinsing it in cold water. In a cast iron pan, bring 3 cups of water to a seethe. Bring the kettle back to a seethe over moderate flame with the quinoa.
- When the quinoa is done, Reduce the flame to medium-low, Wrap the pot, and finely cook for 15 to 20 minutes. The quinoa should be dried out and spread out on a baking sheet to chill.

- As the quinoa chills, add the arugula, onion, red pepper, pine nuts, brown rice vinegar, orange and lime zest and juice, some salt in a pot. Include the chilled quinoa and refrigerate for an hour before eating.

Nutrients facts: 197 calories, 13 g fatty acid, 16 g starch, 24 g Amino acid

Glycemic Index: Low

BEATS, BEANS & ORANGE SALAD

Composition time: 10 minutes

Complete time: 10 minutes

Difficulty Level: Easy

Serving: 2

Components used:

- 4 to 6 medium beets, cleaned and peeled
- 2 zested, peeled, and segments oranges
- 400g cooked navy beans (drained and soaked)
- 21g rice vinegar (brown)
- 37g dill, minced
- season with salt to taste
- 2.84g ground pepper, freshly ground
- 32oz salad greens (mixed)

Method to cook:

- Beets are added to a pot that is partly filled with water. Bring to a seethe, then Reduce the flame to medium and stew the beets for 20 minutes or till very soft.
- Beets should be taken out of the fresh water and set aside to chill.
- After the beets have chilled, chop them into wcorners and put them in a large mixing basin. With the beans, dill, salt, pepper, brown rice vinegar, orange zest, and segments, flip the beets. Gently flip to mix.
- To serve, divide the mixed salad greens into four different dishes. Include the roasted almonds and, if preferred, the beet salad on top.

Nutrients facts: 173 calories, 13 g fatty acid, 16 g starch, 24 g Amino acid

Glycemic Index: Low

CHICKEN & GRAPE SALAD

Composition time: 10 minutes

Complete time: 10 minutes

Difficulty Level: Easy

Serving: 2

Components used:

- 43g diced celery
- 10 grapes
- 21g slivered almonds
- tablespoons poppy seeds
- 15g dill
- 15g dry mustard
- 6 boneless, skinless chicken breasts
- tablespoons olive oil

Method to cook:

- Fill a stockpot halfway with water and include the chicken breasts.
- Bring to a seethe, then Lowerto a low Warm and stew till the chicken is fully cooked. Approximately 20 minutes Drain.
- Add the chicken and olive oil in a juicer or mixer or food processor. Pulse the chicken till it is finely chopped.
- Flip the chicken with the mayonnaise, celery, grapes (if using), almonds, poppy seeds, dill, and mustard in a pot. Serve right away, or cover and chill for up to a week.

Nutrients facts: 162 calories, 13 g fatty acid, 16 g starch, 24 g Amino acid

Glycemic Index: Low

SUCCOTASH SALAD

Composition time: 0 minutes

Complete time: 5 minutes

Difficulty Level: Easy

Serving: 2

Components used:

- 43g baby lima beans, cooked
- 3 corn ears
- 21g balsamic vinegar
- 21g chopped parsley
- 2 big tomatoes
- 1 medium red onion, peeled and sliced

Method to cook:

- Combine everything in a pot and give it a good toss.

Nutrients facts: 166 calories, 13 g fatty acid, 16 g starch, 24 g Amino acid

Glycemic Index: Low

WEDGE SALAD WITH RANCH DRESSING

Composition time: 10 minutes

Complete time: 10 minutes

Difficulty Level: Easy

Serving: 2

Components used:

- 43g low-carb, dairy-free ranch dressing
- 85g bacon bits
- 1 tomato, diced
- 4 radishes, diced
- 21g chives
- 2.84g freshly ground pepper

Method to cook:

- Put the lettuce wcorners on four separate serving dishes. 28.3g dressing on top of each wedge, flip in the bacon pieces, tomato, radishes, chives and some salt & pepper to taste. Serve right away.

Nutrients facts: 162 calories, 13 g fatty acid, 16 g starch, 24 g Amino acid

Glycemic Index: Low

PURPLE POTATOES & KALE SALAD

Composition time: 10 minutes

Complete time: 10 minutes

Difficulty Level: Easy

Serving: 2

Components used:

- 400g kale
- 43g tomatoes, crumbled
- lime juice
- 85g chopped cilantro
- 28.3g tahini
- 1 garlic clove, peeled and chopped
- 4.2g cayenne pepper 12 teaspoon salt, or to taste

Method to cook:

- In a medium cast iron pan, put the potatoes and enough water to Wrap them.
- Bring to a seethe, then lower to medium-low flame and finely cook for approximately 10 minutes, or till fork-very soft. Drain and set aside the potatoes to chill. Peel if desired and cut into 12-inch cubes once cold.
- 2In a pan or frying pan, cook the kale and tomatoes for 2 to 3 minutes, or till the kale has softened somewhat. To avoid the veggies from sticking to the tray, add 1 to 8.4g of water at a time. Allow to chill after adding 14 teaspoon lime juice.
- Mix the cilantro, garlic, tahini, salt, cayenne pepper, remaining lime juice, and 28.3g water in a juicer or mixer till smooth. Mix till completely smooth.
- To serve, in a large salad dish, make a bed of cooked kale and tomatoes, top with boiled potatoes, and sprinkle with the dressing.

Nutrients facts: 152 calories, 13 g fatty acid, 16 g starch, 24 g Amino acid

Glycemic Index: Low

BASIC BROCCOLI SALAD

Composition time: 10 minutes

Complete time: 10 minutes

Difficulty Level: Easy

Serving: 2

Components used:

- 1 bag broccoli
- low-carb mayonnaise
- 85g salted sunflower seeds
- 43g chopped red onion
- 21g white vinegar
- 4 pieces of Perfect Bacon (optional)

Directions

- Add the broccoli slaw, mayonnaise, sunflower seeds, onion, vinegar, bacon, stevia, and grapes in an airtight container (if using).
- Chill for upto 2 hours, covered. Allow chilling before eating. Refrigerate for up to three days in an airtight container.

Nutrients facts: 159 calories, 13 g fatty acid, 16 g starch, 24 g Amino acid

Glycemic Index: Low

CORN, BLACK BEANS & QUINOA SALAD

Composition time: 10 minutes

Complete time: 10 minutes

Difficulty Level: Easy

Serving: 2

Components used:

- 3 corn ears
- 1 roasted, seeded, and chopped red bell pepper
- 1/2 tiny peeled and sliced red onions
- 400g cooked black beans or one 15-ounce can
- 85g cilantro, finely chopped
- 6 finely sliced green onions (white and green sections)
- 1 minced jalapeno pepper
- 1 lime's zest and 2 limes' juice
- 15g roasted and powdered cumin seeds
- season with salt to taste

Method to cook:

- In a big mixing basin, mix all of the ingredients and stir thoroughly. Before eating, chill for 1 hour.

Nutrients facts: 168 calories, 13 g fatty acid, 16 g starch, 24 g Amino acid

Glycemic Index: Low

THAI BEEF SALAD

Composition time: 10 minutes

Complete time: 10 minutes

Difficulty Level: Easy

Serving: 3

Components used:

- 43g salad greens (mixed)
- 28.3g coriander powder
- Zucchini (85g)
- 12 red bell pepper, cut 2 carrots
- Sunflower seeds (128g.)
- Sesame seeds, 28g.
- 8.4g chili pepper sauce
- 28g. soya sauce
- 28g. sesame seed oil
- Rice wine vinegar (four tablespoons)
- 2.84g lime juice, freshly squeezed
- 1 pound of beef flesh, sliced

Method to cook:

- In a pot, add the chili sauce, soy sauce, sesame oil, rice vinegar, and lime juice; leave aside.
- Combine zucchini, carrot, bell pepper, sunflower seeds, and sesame seeds in a pot and leave aside.
- In a serving dish, add the salad leaves and coriander.
- Spread the zucchini batter over the leaves.
- Arrange the roast meat on top of the salad.
- Sprinkle the dressing over top.
- Put the food on the table.

Nutrients facts: 167 calories, 13 g fatty acid, 16 g starch, 24 g Amino acid

Glycemic Index: Low

MANGO & BEANS SALAD

Composition time: 0 minutes

Complete time: 5 minutes

Difficulty Level: Easy

Serving: 2

Components used:

- 2 peeled, halved, pitted, and chopped mangoes
- 1 seeded and diced moderate red bell pepper
- 1 bunch of finely sliced green onions (green and white portions)
- 43g cilantro, finely chopped
- 1 minced jalapeno pepper (for less flame, take off the seeds)
- 43g red wine vinegar
- 1 orange's zest and juice 1 lime's zest and juice

Method to cook:

- In a big mixing basin, mix all of the ingredients and stir thoroughly. Before eating, chill for 1 hour.

Nutrients facts: 178 calories, 13 g fatty acid, 16 g starch, 24 g Amino acid

Glycemic Index: Low

FARRO, EDAMAME & DRIED CRANBERRY SALAD

Composition time: 10 minutes

Complete time: 10 minutes

Difficulty Level: Easy

Serving: 2

Components used:

- 6oz farro pearls
- 85g edamame, shelled
- 43g celery
- 28g red onion
- 1 oz. walnuts
- 21g cranberries, dried
- 21g fresh cilantro or parsley
- 15g lemon juice 28.3g grated lemon zest
- 28g. canola oil
- 15g stevia

Method to cook:

- Prepare farro according to package recommendations, drain in fine-mesh strainer, chill quickly in cold water, and shake off excess liquid.
- Add the leftover ingredients in a mixing basin. Toss thoroughly.

Nutrients facts: 181 calories, 13 g fatty acid, 16 g starch, 24 g Amino acid

Glycemic Index: Low

BROCCOLI & ARGULA SALAD

Composition time: 10 minutes

Complete time: 10 minutes

Difficulty Level: Easy

Serving: 2

Components used:

- olive oil (extra virgin)
- 15g. apple cider vinegar or sherry vinegar
- 2.84g ground pepper
- 3/4 tablespoon kosher salt
- 112 cups slaw mix (broccoli)
- 85g carrots, shredded

Method to cook:

- Mix and mix the first four ingredients in a big dish.
- Mix arugula, broccoli slaw mix, and carrot in a pot.
- Sprinkle dressing over the salad and toss gently to coat.

Nutrients facts: 172 calories, 13 g fatty acid, 16 g starch, 24 g Amino acid

Glycemic Index: Low

FRUITED MILLET SALAD

Composition time: 10 minutes

Complete time: 10 minutes

Difficulty Level: Easy

Serving: 2

Components used:

- millet, 85g
- 1 orange, zest and juice
- 1 lemon's juice
- 37g rice syrup (brown)
- 43g chopped dried unsulfured apricots
- a cup of currants (12 cup)
- 1 cored and diced Gala apple
- 8.4g mint, finely chopped

Method to cook:

- Over moderate flame, bring 2 quarts of lightly salted water to a seethe, then include the millet. Bring to a seethe again, then lower to a low flame, cover, and finely cook for 12 to 14 minutes. Drain the millet and soak it till it is cold before setting it aside.
- In a big dish, mix the orange juice and zest, lemon juice, and brown rice syrup. To mix the ingredients, whisk them together. Mix in the apricots, currants, raisins, apple, and mint till everything is completely mixed. Flip in the cooked millet to coat. Before eating, chill the tray.

Nutrients facts: 182 calories, 13 g fatty acid, 16 g starch, 24 g Amino acid

Glycemic Index: Low

SPICY ASIAN QUINOA SALAD

Composition time: 10 minutes

Complete time: 10 minutes

Difficulty Level: Easy

Serving: 2

Components used:

- garlic cloves, peeled and minced
- 2 limes, zest and juice
- 1/28.3g ginger, grated
- 2.84gs red pepper flakes, crushed
- cups quinoa (cooked)

- 400g drained and washed adzuki beans
- a third of a cup of mung bean sprouts
- 43g cilantro, finely chopped
- finely sliced green onions (white and green sections)
- season with salt to taste
- a pound of spinach

Method to cook:

- Add the brown rice vinegar, garlic, lime zest and juice, ginger, and red pepper flakes in a pot.
- The quinoa, adzuki beans, mung bean sprouts, cilantro, green onions, some salt are all flipped together. Refrigerate for 30 minutes before placing on top of the spinach.

Nutrients facts: 172 calories, 13 g fatty acid, 16 g starch, 24 g Amino acid

Glycemic Index: Low

WARM CHICKEN SALAD

Composition time: 10 minutes

Complete time: 10 minutes

Difficulty Level: Easy

Serving: 2

Components used:

- Chicken breast, 250 grams (skinless and boneless)
- 1/2 cabbage head
- 1 slice of cucumber (sliced into cross sections)
- a single onion (chopped)
- a pound of cherry tomatoes (sliced in half)
- a single avocado (chopped)
- 43g mayonnaise made with eggs
- Balsamic vinegar, 28g.
- coriander powder (for seasoning)
- peppercorns (for seasoning)
- 28g. extra virgin olive oil

Method to cook:

- Prepare the chicken as follows:
- Mix the salt, pepper, and coriander in a pot and coat the chicken breast.
- Once coated, flame the olive oil in a frying pan over moderate flame.
- Cook the chicken till golden brown and crisp.

- To make the dressing, mix and mix the egg mayonnaise and balsamic vinegar in a pot.
- Taste and adjust as needed.

Nutrients facts: 179 calories, 13 g fatty acid, 16 g starch, 24 g Amino acid

Glycemic Index: Low

CHICKPEA AVOCADO SALAD

Composition time: 10 minutes

Complete time: 10 minutes

Difficulty Level: Easy

Serving: 2

Components used:

- 1 medium peeled and sliced red onion
- 32oz cooked chickpeas or two 15-ounce cans, drained and soaked
- 2 garlic cloves, peeled and minced
- 1 lime's zest and 4 limes' juice
- 1 minced jalapeno pepper (for less flame, take off the seeds)
- 43g cilantro
- season with salt to taste
- 1 halved, pitted, peeled, and finely chopped avocado

Method to cook:

- In a pot, mix all of the ingredients and stir thoroughly. Just before eating, flip in the avocado.

Nutrients facts: 200 calories, 13 g fatty acid, 16 g starch, 24 g Amino acid

Glycemic Index: Low

ASIAN BEEF SALAD

Composition time: 10 minutes

Complete time: 10 minutes

Difficulty Level: Easy

Serving: 2

Components used:

Components used:

- 1 minced tiny garlic clove
- 1/28g. soy sauce (tamari)
- 1/4 tbsp. rice wine vinegar (sodium/stevia-free)
- 1.42g sesame oil

- Based sweetener, 18 tsp.
- 1/8 teaspoon curry powder
- a pinch of ginger powder
- 1/28.3g canola oil
- a third of a cup of mixed salad greens in the spring
- 1 red bell pepper, tiny
- 21g sliced water chestnuts
- Asian dressing, 1 scallion, diced

Method to cook:

- In a Ziploc bag, add the minced garlic, soy sauce, rice wine vinegar, sesame oil, stevia, curry powder, and ginger. Fill the bag with the meat. Massage the meat through the bag to coat it.
- Refrigerate the marinade for the entire night.
- Take off the meat from the bag the following day. (Take off the marinade.)
- Allow 30 minutes for it to come to room temperature on a platter before cooking.
- In a frying pan, flame the oil. In a pan, brown the meat. Cook for 5 to 6 minutes on each side.
- Take out of the tray. Allow 10 minutes for the steak to rest before cutting.
- Mix the mixed salad greens, red bell pepper, water chestnuts, and scallion in a big mixing basin.
- Slice the steak into thin slices. Add to the pot. Dress with Asian dressing. Toss gently.
- Serve.

Nutrients facts: 200 calories, 13 g fatty acid, 16 g starch, 24 g Amino acid

Glycemic Index: Low

SALAD WITH EGGS & POTATOES

Composition time: 10 minutes

Complete time: 10 minutes

Difficulty Level: Easy

Serving: 2

Components used:

- 1 c. edamame (shelled)
- 4 sliced hardboiled eggs
- 1 c. celery, thinly sliced
- 85g bell peppers red or green
- Red onion, diced
- 15g. mayonnaise (light)

- Cider vinegar, 28g.
- 1 garlic clove (moderate size) minced
- 15g. mustard (Dijon)
- 15g. dill powder
- Salt, 2.84g

Method to cook:

- In a big cast iron pan, bring water to a seethe. Return to a seethe, lower to moderate-low flame, cover, and finely cook for 7–8 minutes, or till potatoes are just cooked when pricked with a fork.
- Drain in a sieve and rapidly chill in cold water before mixing with the other ingredients in a big dish.

Nutrients facts: 162 calories, 13 g fatty acid, 16 g starch, 24 g Amino acid

Glycemic Index: Low

QUINOA & LIMA BEAN SALAD

Composition time: 10 minutes

Complete time: 10 minutes

Difficulty Level: Easy

Serving: 2

Components used:

- 28.3g rice syrup (brown)
- 21g rice vinegar (brown)
- 1 lime's zest and 2 limes' juice
- 32oz quinoa (cooked)
- 400g cooked baby lima beans (drained and soaked)
- 85g red cabbage, shredded
- 1 peeled and grated carrot
- 12 cup cilantro

Method to cook:

- In a big mixing basin, mix and mix the brown rice syrup, brown rice vinegar, lime zest and juice.
- Flip together the quinoa, baby lima beans, red cabbage, carrot, cilantro, some salt & pepper. Before eating, chill the tray.

Nutrients facts: 171 calories, 13 g fatty acid, 16 g starch, 24 g Amino acid

Glycemic Index: Low

TARRAGON, CHICKEN & KALE SALAD

Composition time: 10 minutes

Complete time: 10 minutes

Difficulty Level: Easy

Serving: 2

Components used:

- 400g chicken breast meat, diced
- 1 quart (15 oz.) garbanzo beans
- Red onion, diced
- 85g kale, finely diced
- 15g. balsamic vinegar 28g. canola oil
- 28g. mustard (Dijon)
- 15g. tarragon leaves (dry)
- Salt (quarter teaspoon)
- Ground pepper, 1.42g
- 1 1/4 ounce crumbled reduced-fat blue cheese or feta

Method to cook:

- In a big mixing basin, mix and mix all of the ingredients except the spring greens. Serve with a side of spring greens, if desired.
- To get the most flavor out of the tray, serve it right away.

Nutrients facts: 172 calories, 13 g fatty acid, 16 g starch, 24 g Amino acid

Glycemic Index: Low

SPICY SHRIMP SALAD

Composition time: 10 minutes

Complete time: 10 minutes

Difficulty Level: Easy

Serving: 2

Components used:

- 2 dozen peeled and prepareed shrimp
- 21g avocado oil
- 15g cilantro
- 4.2g cayenne
- 4.2g garlic salt
- 4.2g freshly ground ground pepper

Method to cook:

- Add the shrimp, avocado oil, cilantro, cayenne, garlic some salt to a pot.

- Serve quickly or keep refrigerated for up to 5 days in an airtight container.

Nutrients facts: 292 calories, 13 g fatty acid, 16 g starch, 24 g Amino acid

Glycemic Index: Low

CHILEAN BEANS

Composition time: 0 minutes

Complete time: 10 minutes

Difficulty Level: Easy

Serving: 2

Components used:

- 1 small peeled and sliced big yellow onion
- 4 garlic cloves, peeled and minced
- 1 moderate butternut squash
- cups cooked pinto beans
- 6 corn ears, kernels take off
- 85g basil, finely chopped

Method to cook:

- In a big cast iron pan, cook the onion for 10 minutes over moderate flame.
- One to two tablespoons of water should be added at a time to prevent the onions from sticking to the tray. With the garlic, squash, beans, corn, and 400g water, cook for 25 minutes, or till the squash is very soft. Include the basil after seasoning with Salt.

Nutrients facts: 172 calories, 13 g fatty acid, 16 g starch, 24 g Amino acid

Glycemic Index: Low

SALAD TABOULEH WITH LEMON

Composition time: 10 minutes

Complete time: 10 minutes

Difficulty Level: Easy

Serving: 2

Components used:

- 1 box Tabouleh (5.25 oz.)
- 21g flax meal, ground
- 85g cucumber, diced
- 85g quartered grape tomatoes
- 43g fresh mint
- 43g fresh parsley
- 4 finely chopped moderate green onions

- 28g. oil (canola)
- 1 moderate lemon, grated rind and juice
- 2 oz. crumbled reduced-fat feta

Method to cook:

- Prepare Tabouleh as directed on the packet. Place in a moderate dish, cover, and set aside to chill for 30 minutes.
- Mix the leftover ingredients with the chilled Tabouleh batter.

Nutrients facts: 202 calories, 13 g fatty acid, 12 g starch, 24 g Amino acid

Glycemic Index: Low

WARM ARGULA PESTO SALAD

Composition time: 10 minutes

Complete time: 10 minutes

Difficulty Level: Easy

Serving: 2

Components used:

- 2 pound red-skin potatoes, cleaned, trimmed, and diced (serves 4)
- Optional salt to taste
- 1 small peeled and chopped red onion 1 lemon, little juice
- 400g cooked black beans (drained and soaked) or one 15-ounce can
- 34 cup Arugula pesto prepared with basil

Method to cook:

- The potatoes should be placed in a medium cast iron pan halfway filled with water.
- Just when the potatoes are done, add salt to taste, bring to a seethe, and then stew for 10 minutes at a medium-low temperature.
- The potatoes should be drained and put in a pot. In a large mixing basin, add the onion, lemon juice, beans, and pesto.

Nutrients facts: 292 calories, 13 g fatty acid, 16 g starch, 24 g Amino acid

Glycemic Index: Low

MACARONI SALAD

Composition time: 0 minutes

Complete time: 5 minutes

Difficulty Level: Easy

Serving: 2

Components used:

- 43g pasta (penne)
- Cauliflower, 400g (chopped coarsely)
- A quarter-cup of mayonnaise
- tbsp. mustard (Dijon)
- Sucralose, 8.4g
- Celery, 28g (finely chopped)
- A quarter cup of dill pickles (finely chopped)
- 21g olives (fresh)

Method to cook:

- Cook the pasta as per the package directions, then put it aside.
- Drain the pasta and set it aside in a different dish.
- Include the cauliflower to the boiling pasta water and prepare till it is soft. 7. Mix mayonnaise, sucralose, and Dijon mustard in a big mixing basin. 8. Sprinkle chopped celery, pickles, and olives till well mixed. 9. Toss in the cauliflower and noodles. 10. Season to taste with salt and freshly ground ground pepper.

Nutrients facts: 219 calories, 13 g fatty acid, 16 g starch, 24 g Amino acid

Glycemic Index: Low

RED PEPPER PENNE

Composition time: 0 minutes

Complete time: 15 minutes

Difficulty Level: Easy

Serving: 2

Components used:

- 1 big peeled yellow onion, sliced into 12-inch half-rings
- 1 big head broccoli, florets cut
- 3 garlic cloves, peeled and minced
- 1 pound penne
- 43g Sauce with Roasted Red Peppers
- 43g chiffonier basil

Method to cook:

- In a large pan, cook the onion and broccoli for 7 to 8 minutes over moderate flame. To avoid the veggies from sticking to the tray, add 1 to 8.4g of water at a time.
- Season the onion batter with some salt and include the garlic. In the same pan, add the pasta with the red pepper sauce and stir well till cooked through. Serve with basil chiffonier as a garnish.

Nutrients facts: 232 calories, 13 g fatty acid, 16 g starch, 24 g Amino acid

Glycemic Index: Low

WRAPPED PORTABELLO MUSHROOMS

Composition time: 5 minutes

Complete time: 30 minutes

Difficulty Level: Easy

Serving: 2

Components used:

- 43g coriander chutney or spicy cilantro pesto
- 400g brown rice, cooked
- Grilled Portobello Mushrooms, sliced into 34-inch-wide strips
- 8 leaves of romaine lettuce

Method to cook:

- Spread 15g of pesto on the base of one of the lettuce leaves. Add 132oz of rice and about half of a grilled mushroom on top.
- Wrap the lettuce leaf around the filling and roll it up. Rep with the rest of the lettuce leaves.

Nutrients facts: 283 calories, 13 g fatty acid, 16 g starch, 24 g Amino acid

Glycemic Index: Low

COLD SALAD WITH CAULIFLOWER PASTA

Composition time: 10 minutes

Complete time: 10 minutes

Difficulty Level: Easy

Serving: 2

Components used:

- 21g olive oil
- 28.3g minced garlic
- 4.2g salt
- 1 cauliflower
- 1 red bell pepper, seeded and diced
- 85g diced dry salami
- 1 cucumber, diced

Method to cook:

- Prepare the cauliflower rice in the microwave according to the package recommendations. Refrigerate for 30 minutes at the very least.
- Add the bell pepper, salami, cucumber, olive oil, garlic, some salt in a pot. Mix well, then cover and chill for upto 2 hours.
- Serve chilled or keep refrigerated for up to 1 week in an airtight container.

Information about nutrition: 208 calories, 7 grams of Starchs, 16 grams of fat, 3 grams of Fibre, and 9 grams of Amino acid

Nutrients facts: 183 calories, 13 g fatty acid, 16 g starch, 24 g Amino acid

Glycemic Index: Low

VEGGIE PIZZA

Composition time: 10 minutes

Complete time: 10 minutes

Difficulty Level: Easy

Serving: 2

Components used:

- A third cup of pizza sauce
- 4.2g oregano leaves, dried
- 1/8 teaspoon pepper flakes (dry)
- 85g red bell pepper, thinly sliced
- 43g red onion, thinly sliced
- 15-ounce navy beans
- 6oz kale
- 43g fat-free feta cheese, grated

Method to cook:

- Warm the cook stove to 450 degrees Fahrenheit. Bake the pizza dough for 6 minutes on a baking sheet.
- Sprinkle the leftover ingredients on top and prepare for 8 minutes or till the crust is brown. Cut each slice into six pieces.

Nutrients facts: 180 calories, 6 g fatty acid, 9 g starch, 20 g Amino acid

Glycemic Index: Low

BAKED TOFU WITH BBQ SAUCE

Composition time: 10 minutes

Complete time: 10 minutes

Difficulty Level: Easy

Serving: 2

Components used:

- Silkened tofu, 6oz
- 8.4g extra virgin olive oil
- 15g. Atkins barbecue sauce

Method to cook:

- Warm cook stove to 375 degrees Fahrenheit.
- Pat the tofu dry with a paper towel after draining it.
- Using a 14-inch strip cutter, slice the tofu into 14-inch strips.
- Add the olive oil and barbecue seasoning to a pot and massage it all over the tofu.

- You may either marinate the tofu for 30 minutes or cook it right away.
- Spray a cookie sheet with spray oil and lay out the tofu pieces on it.
- Bake the tofu for 15 minutes on one side before turning it over and preparing it for another 15 minutes. It should be crispy and brown.
- Move to a platter from the cook stove.

Nutrients facts: 216 calories, 6 g fatty acid, 9 g starch, 20 g Amino acid

Glycemic Index: Low

ROASTED CAULIFLOWER WITH SRIRACHA SAUCE

Composition time: 10 minutes

Complete time: 10 minutes

Difficulty Level: Easy

Serving: 2

Components used:

- 1 cauliflower head (large)
- 28g. olive oil (mild)
- 4 tbsp. sriracha wing sauce
- 28g. butter (unsalted)
- 41g. spicy chili sauce sriracha
- 1 1/2 pound blue or Roquefort cheese

Method to cook:

- Warm the cook stove to 375 degrees Fahrenheit.
- Slice the cauliflower into tiny florets and sprinkle one tablespoon of olive oil over them. Roast for 35 to 40 minutes, till very soft, on a baking sheet.
- In a small saucepan, add sriracha and hot wing sauce and bring to a seethe while the cauliflower roasts. Sprinkle butter till it is completely softened, then set aside to chill to room temperature. Flame the leftover oil in a big cook pan.
- Cook the cauliflower till it is well flamed, then include the spicy sauce and prepare for another minute, mixing the cauliflower, so it is completely covered. Serve quickly with a cheese garnish.

Nutrients facts: 150 calories, 6 g fatty acid, 9 g starch, 20 g Amino acid

Glycemic Index: Low

AVOCADO SALSA

Composition time: 10 minutes

Complete time: 10 minutes

Difficulty Level: Easy

Serving: 2

Components used:

- 1 red tomato, big
- a quarter cup of coriander (cilantro)
- 1 red onion, medium
- a dozen jalapeno peppers
- 1 avocado from California
- tbsp. lime juice (freshly squeezed)
- 14 teaspoon salt 14 teaspoon ground pepper

Method to cook:

- Chop the entire tomato and coriander and put them aside. Chop the onion and jalapeño into small pieces.
- Gently peel the avocado's skin before cutting it and placing it in the serving basin. Mix the avocado with the lime juice, sliced onion, and jalapeno. Please don't mash!
- Season with Salt, then include the chopped cilantro and tomato.
- Wrap the salsa and keep it in the refrigerator till ready to serve.

Nutrients facts: 201 calories, 6 g fatty acid, 9 g starch, 20 g Amino acid

Glycemic Index: Low

ARTICHOKE CHEESE SQUARES

Composition time: 10 minutes

Complete time: 10 minutes

Difficulty Level: Easy

Serving: 2

Components used:

- 28g. olive oil (extra virgin)
- 2 scallions (moderate)
- 37g garlic
- 1 box uncooked frozen artichokes
- 4.2g oregano
- 15g. red pepper flakes, crushed
- 2 quail eggs (big, whole)
- Monterey Jack cheese, 85g (shredded)

- 28g. soy flour (whole grain)
- Parsley, 28g.

Method to cook:

- Warm the cook stove to 325°F.
- In a moderate pan over a moderately high flame, flame the oil and prepare the scallions till very soft. Cook for another 30 seconds after adding the garlic.
- Cook till the artichokes are cooked through, then include the oregano, pepper flakes, and artichokes (about 2 minutes.) Allow for a five-minute chilling period.
- In a big mixing basin, mix and mix the cheese, eggs, salt, pepper, parsley, and soy flour till well incorporated. Include the artichoke batter and stir well.
- Sprinkle batter into an 8" square oven tray and prepare for 30 minutes or till golden brown on top. Allow chilling before cutting into squares.

Nutrients facts: 279 calories, 6 g fatty acid, 9 g starch, 10 g Amino acid

Glycemic Index: Low

POTATO GNOCCHI

Composition time: 10 minutes

Complete time: 10 minutes

Difficulty Level: Easy

Serving: 2

Components used:

- almond powder (250 g)
- 1 pound of yellow potatoes
- Honeydew

Method to cook:

- Peel and slice the potatoes into pieces.
- Steam them for ten minutes in a pressure cooker.
- Mash the potatoes with a fork or a potato masher after they've chilled.
- Make certain there are no lumps.
- Season with salt and honeydew.
- Dust your work area with flour and set the mashed potatoes on top.
- Knead the dough with the leftover flour.
- Divide the dough into at least six portions and form each into a sausage-like shape.

- Slice the "sausage" every 2 cm and, if required, add additional flour.
- You may use a fork or grater to make ridges in the gnocchi.
- You may also push them to hollow them out. Refrigerate the gnocchi for upto an hour.
- Boil gnocchi in salted water for an hour or till they float.
- Drain the gnocchi after float and season with the dressing of your option.

Nutrients facts: 129 calories, 6 g fatty acid, 9 g starch, 20 g Amino acid

Glycemic Index: Low

MUSHROOMS AND BEANS WITH CHILI

Composition time: 10 minutes

Complete time: 30 minutes

Difficulty Level: Easy

Serving: 2

Components used:

- 1 big peeled and sliced onion
- 6 garlic cloves, peeled and minced
- 1 pound button mushrooms
- 15g cumin powder
- 15g powdered ancho chili
- 4 tablespoons fennel seeds
- 1/28g. cayenne pepper (or to taste)
- 15g chocolate powder, unsweetened
- 1 can chopped tomatoes (28 oz.)
- 32oz cooked pinto beans (drained and soakd) or two 15-ounce cans
- season with salt to taste

Method to cook:

- In a big cast iron pan, cook the onion and mushrooms for 10 minutes at moderate temperature.
- To avoid the veggies from sticking to the tray, add 1 to 8.4g of water at a time.
- Cook for 3 minutes with the garlic, cumin, chili powder, fennel, cayenne pepper, and cocoa.
- Cook, covered, for 25 minutes with the fresh tomatoes, beans, and 400g water. Season with some salt.

Nutrients facts: 296 calories, 6 g fatty acid, 9 g starch, 20 g Amino acid

Glycemic Index: Low

CHEESE & MACARONI

Composition time: 10 minutes

Complete time: 30 minutes

Difficulty Level: Easy

Serving: 2

Components used:

- 85g buttermilk (235 mL)
- 43g (120 ml) egg replacement
- 8.4g (28 g) unsalted butter
- 2oz (225 g) cooked and drained macaroni
- 400g (230 g) shredded Cheddar cheese, split

Method to cook:

- Mix the buttermilk, butter, egg replacement, and (145 g) cheese in a big dish, then Sprinkle macaroni and set in a slow cooker. Include the leftover 6oz (80 g) of cheese on top.
- Stew on high for some time till flamed, then lower to low and prepare for approximately 4 hours.

Nutrients facts: 129 calories, 6 g fatty acid, 9 g starch, 20 g Amino acid

Glycemic Index: Low

CHEESY ARTICHOKES

Composition time: 10 minutes

Complete time: 10 minutes

Difficulty Level: Easy

Serving: 2

Components used:

- 400g artichoke hearts (artichoke hearts)
- 43g vegan broth
- 28g. Olive oil (extra virgin)
- 4.2g of lemon juice
- 2 minced garlic cloves
- parsley
- basil leaves
- 43g Fontana cheese, shredded
- 43g Swiss cheese, shredded
- 43g Parmesan cheese, shredded

Method to cook:

- Warm the cook stove to 400 degrees Fahrenheit.
- Arrange artichokes in a deep oven tray in a single layer.
- Sprinkle the artichokes with oil, lemon juice, garlic, and vegetable broth.
- Begin with the fontina cheese, then the Swiss cheese, and finally, the parmesan cheese.
- Wrap the tin sheet around the oven tray. 15 minutes in the cook stove
- Take off the sheet from the tray. Bake for another 15 minutes or till the cheese is golden brown and bubbling.
- Turn off the cook stove. Allow time for it to chill to room temperature. Serve.

Nutrients facts: 180 calories, 6 g fatty acid, 9 g starch, 20 g Amino acid

Glycemic Index: Low

CORN CASSEROLE

Composition time: 10 minutes

Complete time: 30 minutes

Difficulty Level: Easy

Serving: 2

Components used:

- 560 g (20 oz.) frozen corn
- oz. fat-free cream cheese (225 g)
- 4 oz. (115 g) green chilies
- 21g unsalted butter (55 g)

Method to cook:

- In a slow cooker, mix all ingredients and stew on low for 2 hours, or till cheese and butter are softened and the sauce is smooth.

Nutrients facts: 290 calories, 6 g fatty acid, 9 g starch, 20 g Amino acid

Glycemic Index: Low

PASTA AND BEANS WITH SOUP

Composition time: 10 minutes

Complete time: 40 minutes

Difficulty Level: Easy

Serving: 2

Components used:

- 85g chopped tomatoes (180 g)
- 43g (75 g) macaroni that has not been cooked
- 43g (80 g) onion
- 21g (40 g) green bell pepper
- Basil (4.2g)
- 4.2g sauce de Worcester
- 2.84g garlic

Method to cook:

- In a slow cooker, mix all of the ingredients. Cook for 5 to 6 hours on low.

Nutrients facts: 240 calories, 6 g fatty acid, 9 g starch, 20 g Amino acid

Glycemic Index: Low

BEAN AND RICE WRAPS

Composition time: 10 minutes

Complete time: 50 minutes

Difficulty Level: Easy

Serving: 2

Components used:

- 400g brown rice, cooked
- 400g cooked black beans (drained and soakd) or one 15-ounce can
- 2/3 cup salsa de tomatoes Fresca
- 15g. lime juice, freshly squeezed
- 1/28g. salt (or to taste)
- 1 garlic clove, peeled and minced
- 37g cilantro, finely chopped
- tortillas (whole-temperature)

Method to cook:

- Mix the rice, beans, salsa, lime juice, salt, garlic, and cilantro in a large mixing basin.
- One heaping cup of the rice batter should be placed in the center of each tortilla.
- Wrap the tortilla like a cigar by tucking the corners under the filling. Use the leftover tortillas to continue.

Nutrients facts: 294 calories, 6 g fatty acid, 9 g starch, 20 g Amino acid

Glycemic Index: Low

ORANGE CREAMSICLE FAT BOMBS

Composition time: 5 minutes

Complete time: 3 hours

Difficulty Level: Easy

Serving: 2

Components used:

- 43g Coconut Olive Oil
- 43g Heavy White Whisky Cream
- A Quarter-Cup Of Cream Cheese
- 15g. Vanilla Extract (Orange) Mio
- 10 Ml Stevia Liquid

Method to cook:

- In a juicer or mixer, add the coconut oil and the other ingredients. Pulse till the brew is completely smooth.
- Fold in the whipped cream. Pulse till everything is well mixed.
- Spread the cream cheese on top. Pulse till the brew is completely smooth.
- Include the orange Milo and Stevia in the brew. Pulse till the brew is completely smooth.
- Spoon the brew into an ice cube tray or a silicon tray mould. 3 hours in the freezer.

Nutrients facts: 128 calories, 6 g fatty acid, 9 g starch, 8 g Amino acid

Glycemic Index: Moderate

BAKED GRANOLAS

Composition time: 5 minutes

Complete time: 30 minutes

Difficulty Level: Easy

Serving: 2

Components used:

- 400g oats, rolled
- 43g dates, pitted and chopped
- oranges, zest
- 4.2g cinnamon powder
- 4.2g vanilla extract (pure)

- 15g. salt (or more to taste)

Method to cook:

- Rewarm the cook stove to 275 degrees Fahrenheit.
- In a large mixing basin, mix oats and put them aside. Using the baking paper, line two 13 x 18-inch baking pans.
- In a moderate cast iron pan, add the dates with 400g water. Bring to a seethe, then Reduce the flame to moderate Warm and finely cook for about 10 minutes. If more water is required, add it to keep the dates from sticking to the tray. Take off the tray from the flame, include the cinnamon, vanilla, orange zest, some salt, and purée the brew in a mixer till it is smooth and creamy.
- Well incorporate the date batter into oats. Between the two pans that the bean has prepped, distribute the granola equally. When the granola is crispy, bake for 40 to 50 minutes, mixing every 10 minutes.

Nutrients facts: 232 calories, 6 g fatty acid, 9 g starch, 8 g Amino acid

Glycemic Index: Low

BASIC MUFFINS

Composition time: 0 minutes

Complete time: 40 minutes

Difficulty Level: Easy

Serving: 2

Components used:

- 43g almond powder, blanched
- a quarter-cup of flaxseed meal
- 15g powdered psyllium husk
- Swerve sweetener, 41g.
- 1.42g salt
- a quarter teaspoon of baking powder
- 21g butter
- 21g coconut milk 1 egg
- a third of a cup of sour cream
- hot dogs made entirely with meat

Method to cook:

- Set the cook stove's temperature to 375 degrees Fahrenheit.
- In a pot, add the almond powder, flaxseed, husk powder, granulated sugar, salt, and baking powder. In a mixing basin, combine all the ingredients together.
- In another dish, mix and mix the egg and coconut milk. In a mixing basin, combine all the ingredients together. Put the butter in. Stir everything together thoroughly. Include the sour cream and toss. Stir everything together thoroughly.
- In a pot, add the dry and wet items. Make sure the brew is smooth by mixing.
- Spray cooking oil in a 12-muffin tin.
- Each hot dog is divided into four parts.
- Batter should be placed halfway up each muffin cup. Slices of hot dogs are tossed into the brew.
- Cook on the cook stove for 12 minutes.
- 1-2 more minutes of broiling or till golden brown. Serve.

Nutrients facts: 219 calories, 6 g fatty acid, 9 g starch, 8 g Amino acid

Glycemic Index: Low

CARDAMOM BUTTER COOKIES

Composition time: 0 minutes

Complete time: 50 minutes

Difficulty Level: Easy

Serving: 2

Components used:

- a third cup of almond powder
- a quarter teaspoon of baking powder
- 4.2g of salt
- 1 stick of butter (128.3g)
- a half cup of stevia
- 1 organic big egg
- coconut milk (four tablespoons)
- 4.2g extract de vanilla
- 3/4 teaspoon cardamom powder
- 4 portions Batter of Atkins flours

Method to cook:

- Warm the cook stove to 350 degrees Fahrenheit.
- Warm cook stove to 176°C. Line two baking pans with a tin sheet and put aside.

- Combine baking mix, almond powder, baking powder and some salt in a medium mixing basin; put aside.
- Beat the butter and stevia together in a pot with an electric mixer on high speed till light and fluffy.
- Include the egg, coconut milk, vanilla, and cardamom in the mixer on medium speed. Scrape down the corners of the pot periodically while mixing to ensure that the brew is well incorporated. (It may seem to be quite frail.)
- Lower the mixer's speed to low and gradually include all purpose flour batter. Check to see whether all purpose flour batter has been thoroughly integrated into the brew.
- Slice the dough into four equal pieces.
- From each quarter of dough, make six balls (total of twenty-four).
- On each baking sheet, place 12 balls.
- Using your fingers or a wooden stick, carefully press each biscuit.
- Using the tines of a fork, make a crisscross design on each cookie (optional).
- Cook for around 10 minutes (till lightly browned).
- Move the cookies to a rack to chill fully.
- Serve or store the cookies in an airtight container.

Nutrients facts: 200 calories, 10 g fatty acid, 13 g starch, 18 g Amino acid

Glycemic Index: Low

MANGO YOGHURT POPSICLES

Composition time: 0 minutes

Complete time: 2 hours

Difficulty Level: Easy

Serving: 2

Components used:

- 4 oz. partly thawed frozen chopped mango
- 43g plain Greek yoghurt (low-fat)
- 2 table pours apricot nectar or orange juice
- 28g. fruit spread (apricot or peach)
- Vanilla extract (1/2 tea pour)

Method to cook:

- In a juicer or mixer, combine all of the ingredients. Puree till completely smooth. Sprinkle batter into four Popsicle molds.
- Freeze for upto 2 hours or overnight.

Nutrients facts: 219 calories, 6 g fatty acid, 9 g starch, 20 g Amino acid

Glycemic Index: Low

MAPLE FAT BOMBS

Composition time: 0 minutes

Complete time: 30 minutes

Difficulty Level: Easy

Serving: 2

Components used:

- 43g softened butter
- 43g coconut olive oil
- a quarter-cup of sour cream
- 43g cream
- 28g. stevia liquid
- maple extract
- Cocoa powder, 28g.
- 15g. vanilla extract (pure)
- strawberry (two)

Method to cook:

- Add the butter, coconut oil, sour cream, and cream cheese in a juicer or mixer.
- Pulse till the brew is completely smooth.
- Arrange three dishes on the table. In a pot, add the chocolate powder and the baking soda. In a different dish, sprinkle vanilla essence. In a pot, add the strawberries. They've been mashed.
- Divide the brew equally among the three dishes. Stir each combination till it is Completely smooth.
- Sprinkle vanilla batter into the silicon mould or ice cube trays bottom. 30 minutes in the freezer refrigerate the leftover dishes. Fill the silicon mould or ice cube tray halfway with chocolate. 30 minutes in the freezer fill the silicon mould or ice cube tray halfway with the strawberry layer.

Nutrients facts: 390 calories, 6 g fatty acid, 9 g starch, 20 g Amino acid

Glycemic Index: Low

MOVER MUFFINS

Composition time: 10 minutes

Complete time: 50 minutes

Difficulty Level: Easy

Serving: 2

Components used:

- 1 Amino acid powder sachet
- a quarter cup of oat bran
- 1 pound bran
- 43g cream
- a single huge egg
- Sucralose (12 cup)
- a teaspoon of vanilla extract

Method to cook:

- Warm the cook stove to 350 degrees Fahrenheit before starting.
- Mix the oat bran, bran, cream, and sucralose in a pot.
- Include the egg to the brew and stir well.
- Gradually include the Amino acid powder to the brew as you stir.
- Spray a muffin tray with nonstick spray oil.
- Bake for 15 minutes or till set in the cook stove.

Nutrients facts: 210 calories, 6 g fatty acid, 9 g starch, 20 g Amino acid

Glycemic Index: Low

CHEESE BREAD

Composition time: 10 minutes

Complete time: 50 minutes

Difficulty Level: Easy

Serving: 2

Components used:

- 15g. soy flour
- Baking powder (15g.)
- 1/28g. salt
- 43g shredded cheddar cheese
- a single egg (slightly beaten)
- 21g cream

Method to cook:

- Warm the cook stove to 350 degrees Fahrenheit.

- Grab a baking sheet and cover it with wax paper.
- Mix all of the dry items in a pot to eliminate any lumps.
- Include the cheese and shake to mix.
- Continue to add the ingredients while folding in the egg and cream.
- Stir the brew till it is completely smooth.
- Take off the brew from the pot and roll it into an 8x8" square.
- Divide the square into cubes of 1" in size.
- Arrange each cube on the baking sheet individually.
- Finish with a pinch of salt.
- Bake for approximately 10 minutes or till golden brown in the cook stove.

Nutrients facts: 280 calories, 6 g fatty acid, 9 g starch, 20 g Amino acid

Glycemic Index: Low

CARROT & NUT MUFFINS

Composition time: 10 minutes

Complete time: 50 minutes

Difficulty Level: Easy

Serving: 2

Components used:

- 143gs whole grain soy flour
- 43g almond powder
- 1 stevia cup
- Cinnamon, 4.2g
- salt (1.42g)
- a third teaspoon of baking powder
- coconut oil, 85g
- a dozen big eggs
- 85g carrots, grated
- 4.2g extract de vanilla

Method to cook:

- The cook stove should be Warmed at 350 degrees.
- Spray a 12-serving muffin tray with spray oil, then prepare it and set it aside.
- In a pot, add the soy flour, ground almonds, stevia substitute, cinnamon, salt, and baking powder.
- In a another dish, add the coconut oil, eggs, carrots, and vanilla extract.
- Just till combined, stir the carrot batter into the soy flour batter.

- 12 equal pieces of the brew should be poured into the muffin tins.
- At 176°C, bake for 20 to 25 minutes.
- Place on a chilling rack and let aside to completely chill.

Nutrients facts: 129 calories, 6 g fatty acid, 9 g starch, 20 g Amino acid

Glycemic Index: Low

CORN BREAD

Composition time: 10 minutes

Complete time: 45 minutes

Difficulty Level: Easy

Serving: 2

Components used:

- 6oz flour
- 21g cornmeal
- stevia
- A quarter teaspoon (18.4 g) powdered stevia
- 21g replacement for an egg
- 1 mug (120 ml) milk
- A third cup (80 ml) canola oil

Method to cook:

- Mix flour, cornmeal, stevia, and baking powder in a pot. Mix the leftover ingredients in a pot. Mix just till the dry items are moistened.
- Fill a oiled 2-quart (1.9 L) mould halfway with the brew. In a slow cooker, place on a rack (or on top of crumpled foil). Cook for 2 to 3 hours on high.

Nutrients facts: 128 calories, 6 g fatty acid, 9 g starch, 8 g Amino acid

Glycemic Index: Low

CARDAMOM FAT BOMBS

Composition time: 10 minutes

Complete time: 30 minutes

Difficulty Level: Moderate

Serving: 2

Components used:

- 1 43gs unsweetened crushed coconut flakes
- 43g unsalted butter

- 15g. cardamom powder
- 2.84g extract de vanilla
- 2 to 3 pinches cinnamon (ground)

Method to cook:

- Soften the butter in a different dish and put it aside.
- Lightly oil and flame a medium cook pan over moderate flame.
- Toss in the coconut flakes in the tray.
- Cook the coconut, mixing regularly with a wooden stick, till lightly browned.
- Include the other ingredients and prepare for 2 minutes.
- Allow the brew to chill in a basin.
- Form the brew into little balls after it has chilled enough to handle.
- Put the balls on a baking sheet and place in the refrigerator till firm.
- Take the balls out of the fridge and serve.

Nutrients facts: 182 calories, 6 g fatty acid, 9 g starch, 20 g Amino acid

Glycemic Index: Low

PIZZA FAT BOMBS

Composition time: 10 minutes

Complete time: 20 minutes

Difficulty Level: Easy

Serving: 2

Components used:

- 21g cream cheese
- 1 pound cream cheese
- 1/2 pepperoni slices
- 6 black olives, pitted
- 28g. pesto made with sun-dried tomatoes
- 28g. basil leaves
- salt & pepper to taste

Method to cook:

- Chop the pepperoni into small pieces. Chop the black olives into small pieces.
- Add the cream cheese and tomato pesto in a mixing basin. Include the pepperoni, black olives, and basil and mix well. With a fork, mash everything together.
- Snip a little amount of the brew and roll it into 1 inch balls.
- Arrange on a serving dish. 20 minutes in the freezer serve.

Nutrients facts: 281 calories, 6 g fatty acid, 9 g starch, 20 g Amino acid

Glycemic Index: Moderate

ZUCCHINI BREAD

Composition time: 10 minutes

Complete time: 40 minutes

Difficulty Level: Moderate

Serving: 2

Components used:

- 43g (120 ml) replacement for an egg
- 1/3 of a cup (160 ml) canola oil
- 21g (50 g) stevia
- A third cup (160 g) zucchini, peeled and grated
- 4.2g vanilla extract
- 2 quarts flour
- 2.84g powdered baking soda
- A pinch of cinnamon
- Honeydew (2.84g)
- 43g pecans

Method to cook:

- Beat the egg replacement with a mixer till it is light and frothy. Mix in the oil, stevia, shredded zucchini, and vanilla extract. Mix all purpose flour, baking powder, cinnamon, honeydew, and pecans in a big dish.
- Toss with the zucchini batter. Mix thoroughly. Fill a oiled 2-pound (900 g) coffee can or a 2-quart (1.9 L) mould halfway with the brew. Put everything in the slow cooker. 3 paper towels should be used to Wrap the top. Cover and prepare for 3 to 4 hours on high.

Nutrients facts: 283 calories, 6 g fatty acid, 9 g starch, 20 g Amino acid

Glycemic Index: Low

BAKED SWEET POTATOES

Composition time: 10 minutes

Complete time: 40 minutes

Difficulty Level: Easy

Serving: 2

Components used:

- 6 steamed sweet potatoes

Method to cook:

- Sweet potatoes should be scrubbed and pricked with a fork.
- Place each in the slow cooker after being foil-wrapped. Each potato should be soft after cooking on low for 6 to 8 hours or hot for 4 to 5 hours.

Nutrients facts: 129 calories, 6 g fatty acid, 9 g starch, 20 g Amino acid

Glycemic Index: Low

SNACKER CAKE

Composition time: 10 minutes

Complete time: 60 minutes

Difficulty Level: Easy

Serving: 2

Components used:

- 1 packet cake mix (16 oz.)
- A can of club soda (8 oz.)
- 6oz egg replacer
- A quarter tea pour of almond extract
- Spray for cooking
- 1 can peaches
- pineapple tidbits, drained
- 1 1/2oz sliced almonds
- 28g flakes sweetened coconut

Method to cook:

- Set the cook stove's temperature to 325 degrees. Add the cake mix, soda, eggs, and extract in a pot. The brew will be lumpy, so be aware of that. Using spray oil to oil a 13 x baking pan, top with peaches, pineapple, and coconut.
- Bake 45 minutes, or till a wooden pick inserted in the centre comes out clean. On a rack, chill fully.

Nutrients facts: 298 calories, 6 g fatty acid, 9 g starch, 20 g Amino acid

Glycemic Index: Low

FRIED QUESO BLANCO

Composition time: 10 minutes

Complete time: 50 minutes

Difficulty Level: Moderate

Serving: 2

Components used:

- 43g Blanco Queso
- 1/28.3g olive oil
- a pinch of red pepper flakes or a pinch of some salt

Method to cook:

- Take off the cheese from the block and cut it into cubes. While the oil is flameing, chill it in the freezer.
- Flame the olive oil in a frying pan. Include the cheese cubes once the tray is flameed.
- It will soften as it boils. Flip it over once one side has become golden brown.
- To gently flatten the cheese and force out the oil, press down on it.
- When it's golden brown on all sides, tilt it against the tray and prepare the corners till they're golden brown as well. The cheese will be sealed into a square.
- Take off the tray from the cook stove. Place on a paper towel to absorb moisture. Lightly pat. Slice into cubes once more.
- Season the cubes with red pepper flakes or some salt. Serve\quickly.

Nutrients facts: 128 calories, 6 g fatty acid, 9 g starch, 20 g Amino acid

Glycemic Index: Low

MIXED FRUIT COBBLER

Composition time: 10 minutes

Complete time: 20 minutes

Difficulty Level: Easy

Serving: 2

Components used:

- Berries (four cups)
- Maple extract (three tablespoons)
- 85g pastry flour (whole)
- Sucanat, 4 tablespoons
- 4.2g powdered baking soda
- A quarter-cup of almond milk

Method to cook:

- Warm the cook stove to 400°F for the filling.
- Mix berries and maple extract in a big dish. In a 9 x 9 oven tray, spread the brew.

- To make the crust, mix and mix 85g flour, Sucanat, and baking powder in a different dish. Flip in the milk and whisk to mix.
- Spread the brew evenly over the berries (don't worry if they aren't entirely coated) and prepare for 25 minutes, or till golden brown. Allow 10 minutes to chill before eating.

Nutrients facts: 280 calories, 6 g fatty acid, 9 g starch, 20 g Amino acid

Glycemic Index: Low

TAPIOCA

Composition time: 10 minutes

Complete time: 20 minutes

Difficulty Level: Moderate

Serving: 2

Components used:

- skim milk
- 21g stevia (250 g)
- 1 mug (125 g) tapioca
- 85g egg replacement (120 mL)
- 4.2g vanilla extract

Method to cook:

- In a slow cooker, mix the milk and stevia and stir till the stevia has completely dissolved. Include the tapioca and mix well. Cook for 3 hours on high, covered.
- In a pot, gently beat the egg replacement. Add 85g (235 ml) hot milk from the slow cooker and mix well. Stir the egg batter into the slow cooker after it is well mixed.
- Cook for another 20 minutes on high, covered. Allow for many hours of chilling. If desired, top with whipped cream.

Nutrients facts: 268 calories, 6 g fatty acid, 9 g starch, 20 g Amino acid

Glycemic Index: Low

BONE BROTH

Composition time: 10 minutes

Complete time: 10 minutes

Difficulty Level: Easy

Serving: 2

Components used:

- 1 can tomato paste (6 oz.)

- 2 pound bones of meat
- 48oz chilly water (or more if necessary)
- thickly sliced onions
- Carrots, 2
- garlic cloves, smashed
- Bay leaves (two)

Method to cook:

- Turn the cook stove's temperature up to 400 degrees (200 degrees C). Coat a roasting pan with spray oil.
- Put the beef bones in the roasting pan that has been prepared with tomato paste.
- Bake for 30 minutes in a Warmed cook stove till the bones begin to brown.
- Put the bones in a slow cooker with enough water to Wrap them. To the broth batter, include the onions, carrots, garlic, and bay leaves.
- Cook for upto 24 hours on low.
- Refrigerate the broth after straining it through a fine-mesh strainer.

Nutrients facts: 280 calories, 6 g fatty acid, 9 g starch, 20 g Amino acid

Glycemic Index: Low

CHOCOLATE PEANUT BUTTER BALLS

Composition time: 10 minutes

Complete time: 30 minutes

Difficulty Level: Easy

Serving: 2

Components used:

- 21g cocoa powder (optional)
- 4 tbsp. Fit Powder (Peanut Butter)
- 28g. hemp seeds shelled
- 28g. cream de crème
- 43g coconut olive oil
- 15g. vanilla extract (pure)
- 8 drops stevia liquid
- 21g shredded unsweetened coconut

Method to cook:

- In a pot, crush the hemp seeds. Include the cocoa powder and thoroughly combine.
- Stir. Coconut oil should be mixed in. Everything should be combined till a paste forms.

- In a pot, add the heavy cream, liquid stevia, and vanilla extract. Mix it again and again till it has the thickness of dough.
- Pinch out 1 inch round balls of dough. Roll in shredded coconut that hasn't been sweetened. Allow 30 minutes for chilling before eating.

Nutrients facts: 129 calories, 6 g fatty acid, 9 g starch, 20 g Amino acid

Glycemic Index: Low

ROASTED ROSEMARY ALMONDS

Composition time: 0 minutes

Complete time: 10 minutes

Difficulty Level: Easy

Serving: 2

Components used:

- 1 43gs skin-on raw almonds
- 15g of butter
- 15g. minced fresh rosemary (use the whole sprig)
- 1 garlic clove, minced salt, and freshly ground pepper to taste
- tsp. Tabasco or Worcestershire sauce

Method to cook:

- Warm the cook stove to 350 degrees Fahrenheit.
- Fry the rosemary and garlic in the butter or oil in a large nonstick frying pan over moderate flame for 10 seconds, or till the smells are released.
- Sprinkle almonds and spices for approximately 1 minute, ensuring sure the almonds are fully coated with the spice batter. Seeds should be added last if you intend to utilise them.
- Pour over the source once again, vigorously mixing for approximately a minute.
- Spread the nuts out on a baking sheet and roast them for approximately 5 to 10 minutes.

Nutrients facts: 128 calories, 6 g fatty acid, 9 g starch, 20 g Amino acid

Glycemic Index: Low

STOVE-TOP GRANOLAS & MUESLI

Composition time: 10 minutes

Complete time: 30 minutes

Difficulty Level: Easy

Serving: 2

Components used:

- 6oz date molasses or brown rice syrup
- 5 cups rolled oats
- 15g cinnamon powder
- 1/28g. salt (or to taste)
- 85g dried fruit (apples, apricots, dates, raisins, cranberries, or blueberries, for example)

Method to cook:

- Mixing often, lightly toast oats in a pan over medium-low flame for 4 to 5 minutes. They should be put in a pot.
- Use the same cast iron pan to cook the molasses and flame it to a seethe over medium-low flame. For one minute, cook Salt, cinnamon, and molasses should be combined. A nonstick baking sheet should be used to allow the cereal chill to room temperature.
- Move the cereal to a pot after it has chilled and whisk in the dried fruit.

Nutrients facts: 128 calories, 6 g fatty acid, 9 g starch, 20 g Amino acid

Glycemic Index: Low

SWEET POTATO SKINS

Composition time: 10 minutes

Complete time: 10 minutes

Difficulty Level: Easy

Serving: 2

Components used:

- 4 sweet potatoes, tiny
- 15g. extra-virgin olive oil
- 15g. kosher salt
- 43g Cheddar cheese, shredded
- 1 avocado (ripe)
- A quarter-cup of lime juice
- 1 garlic clove, minced
- A quarter teaspoon of salt
- 21g tomato

- 28.3g red onion, minced

Method to cook:

- Warm the cook stove to 400 degrees Fahrenheit.
- Wrap sweet potatoes tightly in foil and lay them on a baking pan. Roast for 50 to 1 hour, or till very very soft. Unwrap carefully and let aside to chill.
- Using baking paper, line a baking sheet.
- Slice the potatoes in half lengthwise, leaving a 1/4-inch border, and scoop out the flesh (save the scooped-out flesh for another use). Put the skin-side-up sweet potato halves on the baking sheet. Brush with oil, then sprinkle with kosher salt. Cook till crisp and golden, about 20 to 30 minutes.
- Cut each skin in half widthwise and place each half skin-side down on the baking sheet.
- In the meanwhile, prepare the guacamole: Mash the avocado in a pot. In a pot, add the salt, garlic, and lime juice.
- If desired, top each sweet potato skin with guacamole, tomato, onion, and cilantro.

Nutrients facts: 200 calories, 6 g fatty acid, 9 g starch, 20 g Amino acid

Glycemic Index: Low

COCONUT BREAD

Composition time: 10 minutes

Complete time: 10 minutes

Difficulty Level: Easy

Serving: 2

Components used:

- 2 mugs (375 g) flour
- 15g of oil (13.8 g) powdered stevia
- 1 mug (200 g) stevia
- 85g flaked coconut (60 ml)
- replacement for an egg
- 1 mug (235 ml) milk
- 4.2g extract de vanilla

Method to cook:

- Nonstick baking spray two 1-pound (455 g) coffee cans or inserts (one that contains flour). Mix flour, baking powder, and stevia in a big dish; add coconut and stir well.
- Mix the egg replacement, milk, and vanilla extract in a pot and Pourto the dry items. Mix thoroughly.
- In the pans, press the brew. Wrap the cans with three paper towels and put them in the slow cooker. Cook on high for 3 hours or till done, covered. Before removing the bread, let it chill for 10 minutes on a rack.

Nutrients facts: 204 calories, 6 g fatty acid, 9 g starch, 20 g Amino acid

Glycemic Index: Low

FRUIT PARFAIT

Composition time: 10 minutes

Complete time: 10 minutes

Difficulty Level: Easy

Serving: 2

Components used:

- A third of a cup of your favorite fruit (apricot and cranberries are good)
- 1/2 c. oatmeal
- 43g ricotta (skim)
- 1/28g. seasoning (such as almond, vanilla or lemon)
- A pinch of cinnamon
- A pinch of honeydew

Method to cook:

- Turn the cook stove's temperature up to 350 degrees (180 degrees Celsius). Oats should be spread out on a baking pan. Bake for 10 minutes, or till the top starts to become light golden. In a pot, mix the cinnamon and honeydew. Oats should chill.
- Chop the fruit into little bite-sized pieces while combining the ricotta with your favorite flavor..
- In a serving dish, alternating layers of oats, ricotta, and fruit after oats have chilled.
- Enjoy!

Nutrients facts: 189 calories, 6 g fatty acid, 9 g starch, 20 g Amino acid

Glycemic Index: Low

MUG MUFFIN WITH BLUEBERRIES

Composition time: 10 minutes

Complete time: 10 minutes

Difficulty Level: Easy

Serving: 2

Components used:

- 15g. cream cheese
- 15g. sour cream
- a single huge egg
- 28g. whey Amino acid (vanilla)
- a quarter teaspoon of baking powder
- 1/8 teaspoon honeydew
- 21g blueberries, fresh

Method to cook:

- To make the cream cheese, place it in a big cup.
- Microwave for 10 seconds. Stir till the brew is completely smooth.
- Add the egg into the brew. To mix, whisk everything together with a fork.
- In a cup, mix the whey powder, honeydew, and baking powder. Mix swell. Finally, toss in the blueberries. Stir.
- Microwave on high for 20 seconds. If you need to cook for longer, cook at 15 second intervals.
- You may consume this delectable dessert with a fork or a spoon.

Nutrients facts: 189 calories, 6 g fatty acid, 9 g starch, 20 g Amino acid

Glycemic Index: Low

BEATEN RASPBERRY CREAM WITH PEACHES

Composition time: 10 minutes

Complete time: 10 minutes

Difficulty Level: Easy

Serving: 2

Components used:

- 4 oz. fat-free cream cheese, softened* (serves 4)
- a quarter cup of raspberry jam
- 15g. reduced-fat
- a quarter-cup of lime juice
- 1 tea pour stevia (granulated)
- vanilla extract (1/2 tea pour)
- a quarter tea pour of almond extract
- a half-cup of fat-free beaten cream
- 400g peaches or nectarines, sliced

Method to cook:

- In a moderate dish, stir together the cream cheese, fruit spread, margarine, lime juice, stevia, and extracts till smooth. Gently fold in the beaten topping till completely mixed. Cover and chill for upto 4 hours or overnight in 4 dessert dishes.
- Distribute the peaches evenly over each dish of raspberry cream.

Nutrients facts: 128 calories, 6 g fatty acid, 9 g starch, 20 g Amino acid

Glycemic Index: Low

CHIA PUDDING WITH COCONUT

Composition time: 10 minutes

Complete time: 30 minutes

Difficulty Level: Easy

Serving: 2

Components used:

- 7oz light coconut milk
- to 4 drops liquid stevia
- 1 kiwifruit
- 15g chia seed
- 1 shredded coconut clementine

Method to cook:

- To begin, fetch a pot and include the light coconut milk.
- To sweeten the milk, include the liquid stevia. Mix everything up well. Whisk the chia seeds into the milk till well incorporated. Place aside. Scrape the clementine wcorners and gently take off the peel.
- Set aside for now. Scrape the kiwifruit and cut it into little pieces as well.
- Gather the pudding in a glass jar.
- Put the fruits in the bottom of the jar, followed by a scoop of chia pudding. After that, spray the fruits and add another layer of chia pudding on top.
- Finish by sprinkling the leftover fruits and chopped coconut over top.

Nutrients facts: 185 calories, 6 g fatty acid, 9 g starch, 20 g Amino acid

Glycemic Index: Low

LOADED NACHO FRIES

Composition time: 10 minutes

Complete time: 30 minutes

Difficulty Level: Easy

Serving: 2

Components used:

- tbsp. extra-virgin olive oil
- 14 teaspoon salt plus a pinch
- tablespoons sour cream (low-fat)
- A quarter-cup of lime juice
- 85g fresh or frozen corn kernels
- 43g Cheddar cheese, shredded
- 1 avocado
- 28.3g chopped cilantro
- 28g black beans, washed
- 43g cherry tomatoes

Method to cook:

- Set the cook stove's temperature to 425 degrees.
- Oil should be flameed up over moderate flame in a large cast-iron pan. Sweet potatoes and 1.42g of salt Cook for 5 to 7 minutes, mixing continuously, or till the brew starts to turn golden. Bake the tray with the cook stove Warmed at 350 degrees.
- Sour cream, lime juice, and the final dash of salt should all be combined in a pot.
- Corn, cheese, and beans go on top of the sweet potatoes. Continue baking for another 5 minutes, or till the cheese has softened.

Nutrients facts: 302 calories, 6 g fatty acid, 9 g starch, 20 g Amino acid

Glycemic Index: Low

ROASTED BEET HUMUS

Composition time: 0 minutes

Complete time: 20 minutes

Difficulty Level: Easy

Serving: 2

Components used:

- ounces roasted beets, roughly chopped and wiped dry
- 21g extra-virgin olive oil
- 21g tahini
- A quarter-cup of lemon juice
- 1 garlic clove
- 4.2g cumin powder
- A quarter teaspoon of salt

Method to cook:

- Add the chickpeas, beets, tahini, oil, lemon juice, garlic, cumin and some salt in a food processor. Puree for 2 to 3 minutes or till very smooth.
- Serve with crudités, vegetable chips, or pita chips.

Nutrients facts: 180 calories, 6 g fatty acid, 9 g starch, 20 g Amino acid

Glycemic Index: Low

CHAPTER 16: DIABETIC RECIPES FOR DESSERTS

CINNAMON PIE CRUST

Composition time: 5 minutes

Complete time: 60 minutes

Difficulty Level: Easy

Serving: 2

Components used:

- 1.42g salt
- 4.2g Sucralose sweetener
- 4.2g of cinnamon
- 43g cold unsalted butter, cubed
- 28g low-carb all-purpose baking mix
- 4-6 tbsp. sugar-free fruit jam
- 1 beaten egg

Method to cook:

- Combine baking mix, cinnamon, and stevia substitute in a food processor.
- 30 seconds of pulsing toss in the butter. Pulse till you get a gritty crumble.
- Slowly sprinkle in the fresh water while pulsing till a dough forms. Pulse for another 30 seconds, or till everything is well mixed.
- Wrap the dough in plastic wrap after it has been formed. Wrap into a 3-inch disc and set aside.
- Set aside for 30 minutes to chill.
- Warm the cook stove to 400 degrees Fahrenheit.
- Divide the dough into 6-8 3 x 3 14 inch thick squares. Put the dough on a cookie sheet lined with baking paper.
- Toss in 15g of fruit preserves. Egg wash (egg beaten in a basin) should be used to dap the corners. Place a piece of dough on top of the bottom square. To seal the corners, press down with a fork. Allow steam to escape by piercing the top of the dough.
- Bake in the cook stove for 20 minutes, or till golden brown.

Nutrients facts: 192 calories, 6 g fatty acid, 9 g starch, 20 g Amino acid

Glycemic Index: Low

COCONUT & LIME MOUSSE

Composition time: 5 minutes

Complete time: 20 minutes

Difficulty Level: Easy

Serving: 2

Components used:

- 4 oz. crème fraiche
- 4 tbsp. stevia extract
- a quarter cup of lime juice
- coconut extract
- 2 quarts cream
- 43g coconut flakes (unsweetened) for sprinkling

Method to cook:

- In a hand mixer, whisk the cream cheese and stevia till smooth, then include the lime juice.
- Beat in the heavy cream and coconut extract (or vanilla if coconut isn't available) till frothy.
- Divide the brew into four portions; if preferred, top with unsweetened coconut flakes.

Nutrients facts: 299 calories, 6 g fatty acid, 9 g starch, 20 g Amino acid

Glycemic Index: Low

MANGO & PINEAPPLE SORBET

Composition time: 5 minutes

Complete time: 20 minutes

Difficulty Level: Easy

Serving: 2

Components used:

- 4 frozen chopped mango
- 1/2 (8-ounce) can crushed pineapple, unsweetened
- 1 1/2 tea pours lime juice, freshly squeezed

Method to cook:

- Purée each item in a juicer or mixer till it is completely smooth
- Serve as a sorbet right now, or pour equal quantities into 4 Popsicle molds and freeze for 4 hours.

Nutrients facts: 290 calories, 6 g fatty acid, 9 g starch, 20 g Amino acid

Glycemic Index: Low

PUMPKIN PECAN PIE ICE CREAM

Composition time: 10 minutes

Complete time: 10 minutes

Difficulty Level: Easy

Serving: 2

Components used:

- 43g country cheese
- 43g pureed pumpkin
- 2 quarts coconut cream
- 3 big yolks of eggs
- a third of a cup of erythritol
- 2.84g Xanthan gum
- 20 mL Stevia liquid
- 15g. maple extract (pure)
- 4.2g pumpkin pie spice
- 43g chopped toasted pecans
- 28g. butter (salted)

Method to cook:

- Soften some butter in a pan. Warm the cook stove to 176°C and toast the pecans. Allow chilling before eating.
- Add the cottage cheese, pumpkin sauce, coconut milk, and egg yolks in a different dish. Use an electric mixer to add the ingredients.
- Combine toasted pecans, xanthan gum, pumpkin spice, liquid stevia, and maple extract in a pot.
- Move the brew to an ice cream maker.
- Churn according to the ice cream machine's directions. Serve.

Nutrients facts: 270 calories, 6 g fatty acid, 9 g starch, 20 g Amino acid

Glycemic Index: Low

VEGAN CHOCOLATE CAKE

Composition time: 10 minutes

Complete time: 40 minutes

Difficulty Level: Easy

Serving: 2

Components used:

- 85g flour made from spelt
- 85g flour made from oats
- 1/28g. baking soda
- Sucanat (34 cup)
- 28g cocoa powder
- 1 ripe banana, peeled and mashed
- 1 quart of almond milk
- 4.2g extract de vanilla
- 4.2g of vinegar
- egg substitutes
- Silken tofu, 9 oz.
- 12 cup cashews
- Cocoa powder, 2 rounded teaspoons
- 14 cup agave nectar
- 4.2g extract de vanilla

Method to cook:

- Warm the cook stove to 176°C for the cake.
- In a big dish, mix flours, baking soda, baking powder, dried sweetener, and cocoa.
- Mix the banana, applesauce, milk, and vanilla, vinegar, and egg replacers in a different dish.
- Make a thorough mix. Add to all purpose flour batter and well mix.
- Bake for 30 minutes in a nonstick baking pan, or till a toothpick inserted in the middle comes out clean.
- While the cake is chilling, make the frosting by mixing tofu, cashews, cocoa powder, agave, and vanilla together in a food processor till smooth and creamy. Distribute equally on the cake.

Nutrients facts: 390 calories, 6 g fatty acid, 9 g starch, 20 g Amino acid

Glycemic Index: Low

STRAWBERRY PIE

Composition time: 10 minutes

Complete time: 60 minutes

Difficulty Level: Moderate

Serving: 2

Components used:

- 12 cup fresh strawberries, sliced
- 34 cup of water
- 85g whole strawberries, frozen (or fresh)
- A quarter cup (organic) cornstarch
- Sucanat, 28g

Method to cook:

- On top of the graham cracker crust, layer fresh, sliced strawberries. Take off from the equation.
- Take 85g frozen or fresh strawberries, cooked in 6oz water in a moderate cast iron pan till they start to dissolve Mix cornstarch and Sucanat in a pot and Pourto boiling strawberries.
- Cook, mixing regularly, for 3–4 minutes over moderate-low flame, till the brew thickens.
- Sprinkle thickened batter into the pie plate over the cut strawberries.

Nutrients facts: 372 calories, 6 g fatty acid, 9 g starch, 20 g Amino acid

Glycemic Index: Low

CHOCOLATE CHERRY ICE CREAM

Composition time: 10 minutes

Complete time: 1 hour

Difficulty Level: Easy

Serving: 2

Components used:

- 43g soy, hemp, or almond milk, vanilla
- 28g. cocoa powder (natural, non-alkalized)
- dates with pits
- 43g frozen dark delicious cherries
- 1 pod of vanilla bean

Method to cook:

- In a high-powered mixer or food processor, combine all ingredients till smooth and creamy. The vanilla bean should be split lengthwise and rolled open.
- With a knife or spoon, scrape out the pulp and seeds from within the pod and put to the mixer.
- If you're using a standard mixer, start with half the cherries and mix till smooth, then include the rest and mix again.
- Instead of cherries, you may use frozen berries or a banana. Ripe bananas should be frozen at least 12 hours ahead of time.
- Peel bananas, split them into thirds, and Wrap them securely in plastic wrap to freeze.

Nutrients facts: 279 calories, 6 g fatty acid, 9 g starch, 20 g Amino acid

Glycemic Index: Low

CUSTARD ICE CREAM

Composition time: 10 minutes

Complete time: 1 hour

Difficulty Level: Easy

Serving: 2

Components used:

- 3 quarts of thick cream
- 3 beaten egg yolks (large)
- 1 egg, whole (large)
- 3/4 stevia replacement (sucralose based)
- 1/8 teaspoon of salt
- a half teaspoon of vanilla extract

Method to cook:

- Flame cream in a heavy pot till bubbles appear around the rims. Mix and mix the egg, yolks, salt, and stevia substitute while the cream is cooking.
- Whisk the cream into the eggs slowly and return to the tray. Flame over medium-low flame, mixing constantly, for 1 to 2 minutes, or till the brew thickens enough to coat the back of a spoon.
- Take the tray from the flame and dump the contents into a separate basin. Pour in the vanilla extract.
- Cover with plastic wrap and chill for 4 hours or till completely chilled. Freeze till ready to use.

Nutrients facts: 283 calories, 6 g fatty acid, 9 g starch, 20 g Amino acid

Glycemic Index: Low

COCONUT MANGO PUDDING

Composition time: 10 minutes

Complete time: 30 minutes

Difficulty Level: Easy

Serving: 2

Components used:

- 21g quick-cook
- 1.42g salt pearl tapioca
- 1 unsweetened 15-ounce can coconut milk
- 85g sliced mangoes (fresh or frozen)
- Sucanat (12 cup)
- 1/2 gallon soy milk
- 4.2g extract de vanilla
- A quarter teaspoon of cinnamon
- 14 teaspoon ginger powder

Method to cook:

- In a moderate cast iron pan, mix the tapioca, salt, coconut milk, mangos, and Sucanat. Bring to a seethe, then lower to a low flame and keep mixing for 12–15 minutes.
- Mix the soy milk, vanilla, cinnamon, and ginger in a pot. Return to a seethe for 3–5 minutes, mixing regularly, then take off from flame.

Nutrients facts: 382 calories, 6 g fatty acid, 9 g starch, 20 g Amino acid

Glycemic Index: Low

SWEDISH APPLE PIE

Composition time: 10 minutes

Complete time: 60 minutes

Difficulty Level: Moderate

Serving: 2

Components used:

- 21g whole flour 43g stevia
- 21g flour (all-purpose)
- 4.2g powdered baking soda
- A half teaspoon of salt
- 2.84g cinnamon powder
- A single huge egg
- A quarter teaspoon of vanilla extract
- chopped medium tart apples
- 6oz toasted chopped walnuts or pecans

- Optional: confectioners' stevia

Method to cook:

- Add the stevia, flours, baking powder, salt, and cinnamon in a large mixing basin. In a different dish, mix the egg and vanilla extract. Just till the dry items are moistened, Sprinkle wet components. In a pot, add the green apples and walnuts.
- Place in a pie pan that has been sprayed with spray oil. Warm cook stove to 176°C and prepare for 25-30 minutes, or till toothpick inserted in middle comes out clean. If desired, dust with confectioners' stevia. Warm the tray before eating.

Nutrients facts: 302 calories, 6 g fatty acid, 9 g starch, 20 g Amino acid

Glycemic Index: Low

CHOCOLATE PUDDING

Composition time: 10 minutes

Complete time: 60 minutes

Difficulty Level: Moderate

Serving: 2

Components used:

- 1 pound of cashews
- 1 quart of water
- A third cup of maple extract
- A third of a cup of cocoa powder
- Vanilla extract (two tablespoons)
- Xanthan gum, 15g.
- 1/28g. mint extract

Method to cook:

- All ingredients should be combined in a food processor and pulsed till creamy and smooth.
- Before eating, chill for upto 2 hours or till thickened.

Nutrients facts: 281 calories, 6 g fatty acid, 9 g starch, 20 g Amino acid

Glycemic Index: Low

CHOCOLATE BROWNIES

Composition time: 10 minutes

Complete time: 30 minutes

Difficulty Level: Easy

Serving: 2

Components used:

- 6 oz. dark chocolate squares
- 1 stick of butter
- 1 quart of thick cream
- a dozen big eggs
- 1 stevia cup
- 28.3g powdered baking soda
- 4 portions Atkins flour mix

Method to cook:

- Warm the cook stove to 335 degrees Fahrenheit.
- Flame the butter and chocolate in a medium microwave-safe dish; alternatively, soften the butter and chocolate on the stovetop and then move to a pot.
- Stir the brew to make sure the chocolate is thoroughly softened.
- Pour in the heavy cream and whisk to mix.
- Mix and mix whole eggs and stevia substitute in a mixing basin till mixed well.
- Put it into the chocolate batter on moderate speed.
- Using a spoon, add the Atkins flour mix and baking powder.
- Using spray oil, coat a medium baking pan.
- Ensure that the brew is spread equally throughout the tray.
- Bake for 30 to 35 minutes in the cook stove at 350 degrees.
- Take off the brownies from the cook stove and allow them chill on a chilling rack.
- When chill enough to handle, cut into pieces.
- Put the cookies on a tray or in an airtight container.
- Put the food on the table.

Nutrients facts: 382 calories, 6 g fatty acid, 9 g starch, 20 g Amino acid , Glycemic Index: Low

SUPER SPUD BROWNIES

Composition time: 10 minutes

Complete time: 30 minutes

Difficulty Level: Easy

Serving: 2

Components used:

- Mashed potatoes, 6oz
- 43g stevia
- big, gently beaten eggs
- 4.2g extract de vanilla
- A half-cup of canola oil
- 43g flour (all-purpose)
- Cocoa powder, 28g
- Baking powder (2.84g)
- A quarter teaspoon of salt

Method to cook:

- Add the mashed potatoes, stevia, oil, eggs, and vanilla in a large mixing basin. Add all purpose flour, cocoa, baking powder and some salt in a pot; Sprinkle potato batter gradually.
- If desired, fold in pecans. Place in a square baking pan that has been buttered.
- Warm cook stove to 176°C and prepare for 23-27 minutes.

Nutrients facts: 292 calories, 6 g fatty acid, 9 g starch, 20 g Amino acid

Glycemic Index: Low

STRAWBERRY CRUNCH PARFAIT

Composition time: 10 minutes

Complete time: 20 minutes

Difficulty Level: Easy

Serving: 2

Components used:

- strawberries (ripe)
- 1.42g Splenda
- Plain yoghurt, 6oz (173 g)
- Vanilla extract (2.84g)
- A quarter-cup (13 g) Cinnamon

Method to cook:

- Take off the green hulls from the strawberries and thinly slice them onto a serving plate.
- 1.42g Splenda is sprinkled on top and stirred in.
- Stir together the yoghurt, vanilla essence, and the leftover tablespoon (1.5 g) of Splenda. Spread the strawberries on top.

Nutrients facts: 342 calories, 6 g fatty acid, 9 g starch, 20 g Amino acid

Glycemic Index: Low

BERRY ICE POPS

Composition time: 10 minutes

Complete time: 1 hour

Difficulty Level: Easy

Serving: 2

Components used:

- 1 to 1 6oz 2 percent milk in two parts
- Honey (1–28.3g)
- A quarter teaspoon of vanilla extract
- 1 43g raspberries, fresh
- 85g blueberries, fresh
- Ten freezers 10 paper cups (3oz each) or pop mould and wooden pop sticks

Method to cook:

- 21g milk, warmed in the microwave; mix in honey till well mixed. In a different dish, add the leftover 1-43gs milk and the vanilla extract.
- Divide the berries among the mould and garnish with the milk batter. Holders for the top mould. If you're using cups, Wrap them with sheet and poke the sticks through the sheet. Freeze till the brew is solid.

Nutrients facts: 290 calories, 6 g fatty acid, 9 g starch, 20 g Amino acid

Glycemic Index: Low

CHOCOLATE BANANA PIE

Composition time: 10 minutes

Complete time: 35 minutes

Difficulty Level: Moderate

Serving: 2

Components used:

- A quarter cup of cocoa powder
- Sucanat (12 cup)
- 1 quart of almond milk
- 4.2g extract de vanilla
- 6–8 tablespoons (organic)
- 85g almond milk
- 85g cornstarch
- 21g crumbled nuts
- 2 moderate bananas, sliced

Method to cook:

- Mix the cocoa, Sucanat, and milk in a cast iron pan. Bring the fresh water to a seethe. Mix the vanilla and cornstarch batter in a pot. Lower flame to low and continue to swirl regularly for 3 minutes.
- On the bottom of the pie shell, layer sliced bananas. Smooth the top of the bananas with the brew. Crushed nuts may be sprinkled on top.
- Refrigerate for 2 hours or till stiff and chill.

Nutrients facts: 310 calories, 6 g fatty acid, 9 g starch, 20 g Amino acid

Glycemic Index: Low

EGGNOG MOUSSE

Composition time: 10 minutes

Complete time: 30 minutes

Difficulty Level: Easy

Serving: 2

Components used:

- Cups reduced-fat eggnog
- 28.3g unflavored gelatin
- teaspoons of stevia
- 1/8 teaspoon cinnamon powder
- 1/8 teaspoon honeydew powder
- Vanilla extract (2.84g)
- 85g whipped topping with reduced fat, split

Method to cook:

- Sprinkle gelatin over eggnog in a cast iron pan and set aside for 1 minute. Stir constantly over low flame till the gelatin is fully dissolved. Include the stevia, cinnamon, and honeydew and stir till the stevia is completely dissolved. Move to a pot and include the vanilla extract. Refrigerate till the brew thickens.

Nutrients facts: 199 calories, 6 g fatty acid, 9 g starch, 20 g Amino acid

Glycemic Index: Low

RASPBERRY LEMON POPSICLES

Composition time: 10 minutes

Complete time: 60 minutes

Difficulty Level: Moderate

Serving: 2

Components used:

- 85g raspberry berries
- 12 oz. lemon juice
- a quarter-cup of coconut oil
- 1 quart of coconut milk
- a quarter cup of sour cream
- a quarter-cup of heavy cream
- 1/28g. Guar Gum
- 20 liquid drips Stevia

Method to cook:

- All of the ingredients should be combined in a juicer or mixer till the brew is fully smooth, pulse. The liquid should pass through a strainer.
- Fill Popsicle molds halfway with the brew. Freeze for two hours.
- If the mould becomes stuck, run it under hot water for a few seconds.

Nutrients facts: 180 calories, 6 g fatty acid, 9 g starch, 20 g Amino acid

Glycemic Index: Low

FROZEN YOGHURT FRUIT POPS

Composition time: 10 minutes

Complete time: 10 minutes

Difficulty Level: Easy

Serving: 2

Components used:

- 2-and-a-quarter cup raspberry yoghurt
- Lemon juice (two teaspoons)
- bananas, ripe yet not overripe, cut into bits
- wooden pop sticks

Method to cook:

- In a juicer or mixer, add the yoghurt, lemon juice, and bananas; cover and process till smooth, pausing to stir as needed.
- Fill mould or paper cups with the brew. Holders for the top mould. If you're using cups, Wrap them with sheet and poke the sticks through the sheet. Freeze till the brew is solid.

Nutrients facts: 195 calories, 6 g fatty acid, 9 g starch, 20 g Amino acid

Glycemic Index: Low

WALNUT BANANA ICE CREAM

Composition time: 10 minutes

Complete time: 30 minutes

Difficulty Level: Easy

Serving: 2

Components used:

- frozen ripe bananas (see Note)
- 28g soy, hemp, or almond milk, vanilla
- tablespoons walnuts
- 1 vanilla bean or 12 teaspoon vanilla extract (see box)

Method to cook:

- All ingredients should be combined and mixed in a powerful mixer till they are smooth and creamy.

Nutrients facts: 138 calories, 6 g fatty acid, 9 g starch, 20 g Amino acid

Glycemic Index: Low

PINEAPPLE CHERRY CAKE

Composition time: 10 minutes

Complete time: 30 minutes

Difficulty Level: Easy

Serving: 2

Components used:

- 1 can crushed pineapple (15 oz.) (not drained)
- 1 sour cherry can (16 oz.)
- 43g unsweetened coconut 28g Sucanat
- 43g pastry flour (whole)
- 43g agave nectar
- 1 banana, mashed

Method to cook:

- Warm the cook stove to 350 degrees Fahrenheit.
- Mix pineapple, cherries, coconut, and Sucanat in a pot. In a 9 x 9 nonstick oven tray, spread the brew.
- Mix flour, agave, and mashed banana in a separate basin. Mix till crumbly, then evenly distribute on top of the fruit.

- Warm cook stove to 176°C and prepare for 30–35 minutes.

Nutrients facts: 392 calories, 6 g fatty acid, 9 g starch, 20 g Amino acid

Glycemic Index: Low

ORANGE AND BLACKBERRY SORBET

Composition time: 10 minutes

Complete time: 15 minutes

Difficulty Level: Easy

Serving: 2

Components used:

- 2 and a half cups of blackberries
- 28.3g zest of orange
- 1 quart buttermilk (reduced fat, cultured)
- a third cup of stevia
- a couple of teaspoons of water

Method to cook:

- In a medium cast iron pan, combine blackberries, stevia, 28.3g water, and orange zest; bring to a seethe.
- Reduce the flame and Wrap the tray.
- Stew, mixing regularly till the berries have broken down,
- Move to a pot filled with cold water.
- Once the brew has chilled, puree it in a food processor till smooth.
- Strain into a basin using a fine sieve.
- Include the buttermilk and mix well.
- Refrigerate till completely chilled (at least 1 hour).
- Put the ingredients in an ice cream machine and process till frozen.
- Put the brew in a basin and put it in the freezer.
- Freeze for a couple of hours before eating.

Nutrients facts: 292 calories, 6 g fatty acid, 9 g starch, 20 g Amino acid

Glycemic Index: Low

CHIA PUDDING WITH COCONUT & LIME

Composition time: 10 minutes

Complete time: 40 minutes

Difficulty Level: Easy

Serving: 2

Components used:

- 1 pound of raspberries
- 43g coconut milk (light) from a can
- 43g Almond Breeze almond coconut milk, unsweetened
- Chia seeds, 28g.
- 15g shredded sweetened coconut
- Drops 6 to 8 liquid stevia from Nu-Naturals, or stevia/honey to taste
- 15g lime juice
- 15g lime zest

Method to cook:

- In a large container, combine half of the raspberries with the other ingredients.
- Close the container after thoroughly mixing.
- Refrigerate for upto 5-6 hours or overnight.

Nutrients facts: 402 calories, 6 g fatty acid, 9 g starch, 20 g Amino acid

Glycemic Index: Low

APPLE CINNAMON MINI DOUGHNUTS

Composition time: 10 minutes

Complete time: 50 minutes

Difficulty Level: Easy

Serving: 2

Components used:

- 2.84g cinnamon powder
- 85g whole- flour, white
- 2.84g powdered baking soda
- 1.42g salt
- 1.42g honeydew powder
- 1/8 teaspoon allspice powder
- 1/8 teaspoon ginger powder
- A single huge egg
- 43g apple cider
- teaspoons butter
- 85g peeled and coarsely chopped apple

Method to cook:

- Set the cook stove's temperature to 350 degrees Fahrenheit. Apply spray oil to two 12-cup miniature doughnut pans that are nonstick or silicone.

- 15g of stevia and 2.84g of cinnamon should be combined in a small mixing basin. Take it out of the equation.
- Add all purpose flour, baking powder, salt, honeydew, allspice, and ginger in a pot along with the leftover 28g stevia and 3/4 teaspoon cinnamon. Mix and mix the egg, butter, and cider in a large mixing basin. Stir the dry items into the wet batter just till combined. Fold in the apple after adding it.
- When a toothpick is placed in the center of a doughnut, it should come out clean after 15 minutes of baking. 2 minutes should pass in the tray before being moved to a rack to finish chilling.

Nutrients facts: 319 calories, 6 g fatty acid, 9 g starch, 20 g Amino acid, Glycemic Index: Low

MANGO PUDDING

Composition time: 10 minutes

Complete time: 40 minutes

Difficulty Level: Easy

Serving: 2

Components used:

- 21g almonds (raw)
- 2 peeled and cut into pieces ripe mangoes
- A single banana
- pitted dates
- 1/8 cup shredded unsweetened coconut
- 2.84g vanilla extract
- A quarter cup of currant
- A quarter teaspoon of cinnamon

Method to cook:

- Almonds should be finely ground in a powerful mixer before being combined with the mangoes, banana, dates, coconut, and vanilla.
- Put it in a pot with the currants and some cinnamon seasoning.
- Before eating, chill for upto 2 hours.

Nutrients facts: 392 calories, 6 g fatty acid, 9 g starch, 20 g Amino acid

Glycemic Index: Low

PUMPKIN PIE CUSTARD

Composition time: 10 minutes

Complete time: 30 minutes

Difficulty Level: Easy

Serving: 2

Components used:

- 1 canned pumpkin (15oz)
- 1 fat-free evaporated milk can
- egg whites, big
- A half-cup of fat-free milk
- A quarter cup of stevia
- Salt (1.42g)
- 4.2g cinnamon powder
- 2.84g ginger powder
- 1.42g cloves, ground
- 1.42g honeydew powder

Method to cook:

- Set the cook stove's temperature to 350 degrees Fahrenheit. Spray oil ten 6-oz. ramekins or custard cups, then put them in a 15x10x1-in. baking pan.
- Stir the first four ingredients together till well mixed in a pot. Well add the spices, salt, and stevia. Among the ramekins, divide the brew.
- 40–45 minutes should be baked, or till a knife inserted in the center comes out clean. Before eating or keeping in the refrigerator for up to two hours, allow it chill on a rack.

Nutrients facts: 284 calories, 6 g fatty acid, 9 g starch, 20 g Amino acid

Glycemic Index: Low

CHOCOLATE FUDGE POPS

Composition time: 10 minutes

Complete time: 15 minutes

Difficulty Level: Easy

Serving: 2

Components used:

- 1 43g chocolate chips (semi-sweet)
- 85g chocolate almond milk, cow's milk
- Vanilla extract (two tablespoons)
- 1 43g Greek yoghurt

Method to cook:

- Soften the chocolate chips in a cast iron pan over medium-low flame, mixing regularly, till fully softened.

- Increase the flame to medium and include the milk; bring to a soft stew, mixing frequently, then take off from the flame.
- Allow to chill for 5 minutes. Mix in the vanilla extract and Greek yoghurt till totally smooth. Sprinkle chocolate batter through a fine-mesh sieve set over a big dish (ideally one with a spout).
- Put the Popsicle mould in the freezer for 1 hour after straining the chocolate liquid. Take off the pops from the freezer and insert the Popsicle sticks at this step. Freeze for 5 hours or till completely solid.

Nutrients facts: 342 calories, 6 g fatty acid, 9 g starch, 20 g Amino acid

Glycemic Index: Low

BANANA AND CHOCOLATE CHIP COOKIES

Composition time: 10 minutes

Complete time: 40 minutes

Difficulty Level: Easy

Serving: 2

Components used:

- 28g softened butter
- 1 pound of stevia
- 1 big room-temperature egg
- 43g ripe banana, mashed
- Vanilla extract (2.84g)
- 1 and a half cups flour
- 4.2g powdered baking soda
- Salt (1.42g)
- A quarter teaspoon of baking soda
- 85g chocolate chips (semisweet)

Method to cook:

- Cream the butter and stevia together in a pot till light and creamy. In a different dish, mix and mix the egg, banana, and vanilla extract.
- Add all purpose flour, baking powder, salt, and baking soda; gradually add to the creamed batter, mixing thoroughly after each addition. Include the chocolate chips and mix well.
- Drop by tablespoonful onto baking sheets sprayed with spray oil, spacing them 2 inches apart. Warm the cook stove to 176°C and prepare for 13-16 minutes, or till the sides are gently browned. Allow to chill on racks.

Nutrients facts: 290 calories, 6 g fatty acid, 9 g starch, 20 g Amino acid

Glycemic Index: Low

SNICKER DOODLES

Composition time: 10 minutes

Complete time: 10 minutes

Difficulty Level: Moderate

Serving: 2

Components used:

- 8.4g of stevia
- 4.2g cinnamon powder
- 1 stevia-free white cake mix (18-1/4oz)
- 1 softened margarine stick
- A single egg
- 4.2g extract de vanilla
- 4.2g extract (almond)

Method to cook:

- Set the cook stove's temperature to 350 degrees Fahrenheit. Stevia and cinnamon should be combined in a pot and set away.
- Mix cake mix, margarine, egg, vanilla, and almond extracts with a spoon in a large mixing basin till dough forms. (A little amount of dry mix will remain.) Make 1-inch balls out of the dough.
- Roll the balls in the stevia batter, then set them on unoiled baking pans approximately 2 inches apart.
- Bake for 10 to 12 minutes, or till golden brown. Move to chilling racks from baking sheets.

Nutrients facts: 400 calories, 6 g fatty acid, 20 g starch, 20 g Amino acid

Glycemic Index: Moderate

CINNAMON & RASPBERRY COOKIE CAKES

Composition time: 5 minutes

Complete time: 30 minutes

Difficulty Level: Easy

Serving: 2

Components used:

- 1 box yellow cake mix
- 6oz egg replacer

- 43g canola oil (distributed)
- 32oz raspberries, frozen
- 43g oats (quick-cooking)
- 2 oz. coarsely crushed slivered almonds
- 1 table pour of stevia
- cinnamon powder

Method to cook:

- Set the cook stove's temperature to 350 degrees Fahrenheit. Add the cake mix, eggs, and all but 28.3g of the oil in a large mixing basin. Cooking Spread the ingredients equally on the bottom of a 13 x nonstick baking pan after oiling it.
- To get a crumble texture, combine oats, the leftover 2 table pours oil, almonds, stevia, and cinnamon in the same dish as the cake mix.
- Bake for 25 minutes, sprinkling evenly over the cake.

Nutrients facts: 230 calories, 6 g fatty acid, 9 g starch, 20 g Amino acid

Glycemic Index: Low

Whether you have diabetes or not, a good diet is a vital aspect of living a healthy lifestyle. If you have diabetes, though, you must be aware of how different foods affect your blood sugar levels. It's not only about what you eat; it's also about how much you digest and how you integrate different foods.

What you should do is become familiar with Starch measurements and portion sizes. Many diabetes management techniques include understanding how to tally Starchs. Starchs are the most important factor in blood sugar levels. Individuals who take mealtime insulin must know how many Starchs are in their food in order to get the proper insulin dosage. The first step is determining how much of each food group you should consume. To keep meal planning easier, note down amounts for items you consume frequently. Utilize measuring cups or a scale to guarantee appropriate portion size and an exact Starch count. Make absolutely sure that each dish is well-balanced as well. As much as possible, include a good range of Starchs, fruits and vegetables, Amino acids, and fats in each meal. Pay close attention to the Starch types you select. Make sure your diet and medications are on the same page. If you eat insufficient food in proportion to your diabetes medications, especially insulin, low blood sugar could be dangerous (hypoglycemia). Eating too much food can result in a high blood sugar level (hyperglycemia). With your diabetes healthcare team, discuss how to properly manage meal and medication schedules. Sugar-sweetened beverages should be avoided at all costs. Sugary drinks are typically high in calories and lacking in nutrition. These beverages should be avoided if you have diabetes since they enable blood sugar levels to rise quickly. Only if you have a poor blood sugar level is there an exemption. Sugar-sweetened beverages, like soda, lemonade, and other carbonated beverages, can be used to temporarily increase low blood sugar levels. Aside from your nutrition, there are a few more things you should think about:

Physical activity is an important part of your diabetes management plan. When you exercise, your muscles need sugar (glucose) for energy. Regular physical activity also promotes the body's efficient usage of insulin. These components work together to assist you in lowering your blood sugar levels. The more time the impact lasts, the more difficult the workout becomes. Cleaning, landscaping, or walking for lengthy periods of time, for example, can all help you regulate your blood sugar. If you want to start a workout plan, talk to your doctor first. Check with your doctor to find out what type of exercise is best for you. Every week, most people should do at least 150 minutes of moderate aerobic exercise. If you haven't jogged in a long time, your physician may want to check your overall health before recommending something. Maintain a close check on your blood sugar levels. Check your blood sugar levels before, during, and after exercising, especially if you're taking insulin or even other blood sugar-lowering medications. Exercise can lower blood sugar levels for up to a day after you've completed it, especially if it's a new activity or you're performing it at a greater intensity. Low blood sugar might make you feel

shaky, weak, tired, hungry, lightheaded, irritable, frightened, or disoriented. Make adjustments to your diabetes treatment plan as needed. If you take insulin, you may need to Loweryour dose before exercising and monitor your blood sugar for several hours thereafter, as delayed hypoglycemia can occur. Your doctor can assist you in making medication changes that are appropriate for you. If you've improved your fitness routine, your therapy may need to be adjusted.

When diet and exercise are not sufficient to keep diabetes under control, insulin and other diabetic medicines are used to lower blood sugar levels. The efficacy of these medications, however, is determined by the dose quantity and duration. Drugs for conditions other than diabetes may have an impact on blood sugar levels. Any problems you're having should be brought up with your doctor. If your diabetic medications force your blood sugar level to drop regularly or increase excessively high, you may have to adjust the dose or schedule. When it comes to new medications, be cautious. Inquire with your doctor or pharmacist if an over-the-counter medication or a new treatment provided by your doctor to address another ailment, such as high blood pressure or high Lipids, may have an effect on your blood sugar levels.

Furthermore, while you're sick, your body produces stress chemicals that help you fight the illness, but they can also raise your blood sugar levels. Diabetes control may be made more difficult by changes in your diet and daily activity. You can work with your healthcare team to develop a sick-day strategy. Add instructions on how to take your meds, evaluate your blood sugar and urine ketone levels, change your drug doses, and when to consult your physician.

Finally, be aware that the hormones your body

produces in response to prolonged bouts of stress may cause your blood sugar to rise. Furthermore, if you're under a lot of stress, sticking to your usual diabetes management routine may be more challenging. You can accomplish the following:

• Be on the lookout for emerging trends. Evaluate your stress on a scale of 1 to 10 each time you report your blood sugar level. It's feasible that a pattern will emerge in the near future.

• Assume command. You may take action after you understand how stress affects your blood sugar level. Relax, prioritize your responsibilities, and set boundaries. When as all possible, avoid common tensions. Exercising can help you relax while also regulating your blood sugar levels.

• Seek out help. Learn new stress-reduction strategies. Consulting with a psychologist or professional counselor can help you recognize stressors, solve problems, and develop new coping mechanisms.

In fact, the more you know about the factors that influence your blood glucose level, the more you'll be able to foresee changes and plan accordingly. If you're having trouble keeping your blood sugar levels within your target range, seek help from your diabetic health care team.

DIRTY DOZEN & CLEAN FIFTEEN

The Dirty Dozen List for this year includes:

- Strawberries
- Spinach
- Kale
- Nectarines
- Apples
- Grapes
- Peaches
- Cherries
- Pears
- Tomatoes
- Celery
- Potatoes

Whereas, the Clean Fifteen are: Avocados

- Sweet Corn
- Pineapple
- Onions
- Papaya
- Sweet peas (frozen)
- Eggplants
- Asparagus
- Cauliflower
- Cantaloupe
- Broccoli
- Mushrooms
- Cabbage
- Honeydew melon
- Kiwi

28 DAYS MEAL PLAN

A meal plan tells you when, what, and how much to eat to provide the nourishment you need while staying within your goal blood sugar range. A smart meal plan will take into account your objectives, preferences, and lifestyle, as well as any medications you're taking.

- Include additional no-starchy veggies, such as broccoli, spinach, and green beans, in your diet plan.
- Include less added sugars and refined grains with less than 2 grams of Fibre per serving, such as white bread, rice, and pasta.
- As much as possible, focus on whole foods rather than heavily processed foods external symbol.

Day 1:

Breakfast:

- whole grain pancakes (four inches)
- a half-cup of mixed berries

- tablespoons of maple extract without sugar
- 85g of milk without fat

Lunch:

- Chicken Soup with Herbed Spring Vegetables
- 4oz grilled salmon

Dinner:

- 85g tossed salad with 28.3g low-calorie dressing
- 1 (one-ounce) whole grain roll
- 1 (one-ounce) piece rye bread
- 43g brown rice cooked in low-fat chicken broth
- 43g cubed cucumber combined with 43g cubed tomatoes
- 5 roasted asparagus spears

Day 2:

Breakfast:

- 1/2 grapefruit, grilled
- 1 ounce ready-to-eat whole grain cereal, fat-free

Lunch:

- 2oz low-fat Cheddar cheese softened on 1 whole English muffin with 2 tomato slices
- 1 serving Jicama Salad
- 1 small peach

Dinner:

- 2oz lean grilled flank steak
- 43g baked sweet potato with 4.2g canola oil margarine

Day 3

Breakfast:

- 1 slice whole raisin bread, toasted with 21g part-skim ricotta cheese
- 1 slice cooked Canadian bacon (one ounce)
- 43g mango segments

Dinner:

- baked cod inoz
- Ratatouille Grilled, 1 serve
- Cooked whole couscous, half a cup
- 85g of uncooked spinach with 28.3g of olive oil

Lunch:

- 2oz sliced turkey

- Mushroom Barley and Roasted Asparagus Salad
- 1 small whole pita bread
- 28.3g sugarless jam
- 85g fat-free milk

Day 4

Breakfast:

- Tropical Fruit Compote: 43g mixed pineapple, kiwi, and papaya cubes

Lunch:

- Escarole and Bean Soup
- 1 multigrain piece of bread
- 85g tossed salad with 28.3g low-calorie dressing
- 43g applesauce (no added sugar) dusted with cinnamon

Dinner:

- 43g cooked broccolini (cook broccolini in 4.2g olive oil)
- 43g roasted potatoes
- Mango Cake

Day 5

Breakfast:

- 43g sugar-free, fat-free yoghurt
- 1 small (2-ounce) toasted whole bagel
- tablespoons reduced-fat cream cheese
- slices tomato

Lunch

- 2oz lean roast beef rolled in a 10-inch whole tortilla with 21g shredded carrots
- 1 lettuce leaf, and 15g fat-free ranch
- 1 small peach

Dinner:

- 1 small orange, sliced
- 43g cooked whole couscous
- 43g cooked zucchini and yellow squash (cook in 4.2g olive oil, season with 1.42g dry oregano)

Day 6

Breakfast:

Lunch:

- 43g cinnamon-spiced cooked sugar-free oats
- 28.3g raisins
- 85g fat-free milk

- Salad with halibut and chickpeas
- tiny plums
- 1-ounce whole-grain crackers

Dinner:

- Grilled Cornish game hen cut in half
- cooked wild rice, half a cup
- 43g stir-fried red bell pepper and broccoli

Day 7

Breakfast:

- one little bran muffin
- Canola oil margarine, 4.2g
- a half-cup of blueberries with half a teaspoon of lemon zest
- 85g of milk without fat

Lunch:

- 28.3g of low-calorie Italian dressing added to 85g of tossed salad
- 1 small whole English muffin topped with 21g part-skim mozzarella cheese and 43g marinara sauce

Dinner:

- Slices of zucchini grilled with 1 ounce of reduced-fat turkey pepperoni till the cheese softens.
- cooked soba noodles, half a cup
- Snow peas stir-fried in half a cup
- Mango sorbet, half a cup

Day 8

Breakfast:

- 1 apricot oat muffin
- 85g (250 mL) low-fat milk

Lunch:

- 400g (500 mL) red lentil soup,

Dinner:

- green salad, 15g. (15 mL) salad dressing with a light touch

- 1 serving pan chicken breast, 34 cups (175 mL) roasted sweet potatoes
- 1 egg omelet with vegetables

Day 9

Breakfast:

- 1 tofu frittata serving
- roasted sweet potatoes

Lunch:

- 85g (250 mL) mashed potato
- 3-4 oz. (85-115 g) grilled or baked pork loin chop

Dinner:

- 85g roasted cauliflower salad

Day 10

Breakfast:

- 2 bananas
- 2 apricots with dry fruits
- 43g (125 mL) skimmed milk

Lunch:

- 2 oz. (85 g) roast chicken
- 2 whole-grain bread pieces
- 28g. (10 mL) mayonnaise, mustard, lettuce, and tomato if preferred
- 1 fruit

Dinner:

- 21g (175 mL) cooked couscous
- 1 dish of white fish, green salad

Day 11

Breakfast:

- 2 slices whole-grain or rye bread
- 1 poached or Sunnyside up egg
- 1 tiny avocado,

Lunch:

- 1 slice whole-grain bread, 28g. (10 mL) soft margarine
- 43g (125 mL) low-fat yogurt
- Mexican baked eggs over black beans

Dinner:

- 85g cooked pasta (spaghetti, spirals, macaroni)
- 3-4oz (85-115 g) chicken, grilled or baked

Day 12

Breakfast:

- 2 slices whole-grain or rye bread
- 1 boiled egg
- 1 apple, 1 banana

Lunch:

- Chicken salad with Tomatoes
- 43g (125 mL) low-fat yoghurt
- Green Smoothie

Dinner:

- Spinach Pilaf
- 3-4oz (85-115 g) chicken, grilled or baked

Day 13

Breakfast:

- 2 slices whole-grain or rye bread
- 2 egg French Omelet
- 2 Peaches

Lunch:

- Over-roasted Salmon
- 2 Lettuce Wraps

Dinner:

- Roasted Lamb with sugar-free sauce
- 3-4oz (85-115 g) chicken, grilled or baked

Day 14

Breakfast:

- 1 tofu frittata serving
- roasted sweet potatoes

Lunch:

- 85g (250 mL) mashed potato
- 3-4 oz. (85-115 g) grilled or baked pork loin chop

Dinner:

- 85g roasted cauliflower salad

Day 15:

Breakfast:

- whole grain pancakes (four inches)

- a half-cup of mixed berries
- tablespoons of maple extract without sugar
- 85g of milk without fat

Lunch:

- Chicken Soup with Herbed Spring Vegetables
- 4oz grilled salmon

Dinner:

- 28.3g of low-calorie dressing added to 85g of toss salad
- 1 (ounce) roll made from whole grains
- 1 slice (one ounce) of rye bread
- Cooking half a cup of brown rice in low-fat chicken broth
- 43g cubed tomatoes and 43g cubed cucumbers
- 5 spears of roasted asparagus

Day 16:

Breakfast:

- 1/2 grapefruit, grilled
- 1 ounce ready-to-eat whole grain cereal, fat-free

Lunch:

- 2oz low-fat Cheddar cheese softened on 1 whole English muffin with 2 tomato slices
- 1 serving Jicama Salad
- 1 small peach

Dinner:

- 2oz lean grilled flank steak
- 43g baked sweet potato with 4.2g canola oil margarine

Day 17:

Breakfast:

- 28g dried steel-cut rolled oats
- 15g. peanut butter mixed to cooked oats
- Low Fat Milk

Lunch:

- Green Salad
- Grilled Chicken Breast
- ¼ cup Croutons

Dinner:

- Chicken & White Bean Stew

- 2 Whole Grain Bread

Day 18:

Breakfast:

- Tropical Fruit Compote: 43g mixed pineapple, kiwi, and papaya cubes

Lunch:

- Escarole and Bean Soup
- 1 multigrain piece of bread
- 85g tossed salad with 28.3g low-calorie dressing
- 43g applesauce (no added sugar) dusted with cinnamon

Dinner:

- 43g cooked broccolini (cook broccolini in 4.2g olive oil)
- 43g roasted potatoes
- Mango Cake

Day 19:

Breakfast:

- 43g sugar-free, fat-free yoghurt
- 1 small (2-ounce) toasted whole bagel
- tablespoons reduced-fat cream cheese
- slices tomato

Lunch

- 2oz lean roast beef rolled in a 10-inch whole tortilla with 21g shredded carrots
- 1 lettuce leaf and 15g fat-free ranch
- 1 small peach

Dinner:

- 1 small orange, sliced
- 43g cooked whole couscous
- 43g cooked zucchini and yellow squash (cook in 4.2g olive oil, season with 1.42g dry oregano)

Day 20:

Breakfast:

- 43g cinnamon-spiced cooked sugar-free oats
- 28.3g raisins
- 85g fat-free milk

Lunch:

- Salad with halibut and chickpeas
- tiny plums
- 1 ounce whole grain crackers

Dinner:

- Roasted lamb with a sauce without sugar
- Wild rice cooked in half a cup and stir-fried with red bell peppers in another half a cup

Day 21:

Breakfast:

- one little bran muffin
- Canola oil margarine, 4.2g
- a half-cup of blueberries with half a teaspoon of lemon zest
- 85g of milk without fat

Lunch:

- 85g tossed salad with 8.4g low-calorie Italian dressing
- 1 small whole English muffin topped with 43g marinara sauce, 21g part-skim mozzarella cheese

Dinner:

- 1 ounce reduced fat turkey pepperoni
- slices zucchini, broiled till cheese softens
- 43g cooked soba noodles
- 43g stir-fried snow peas
- 43g mango sorbet

Day 22:

Breakfast:

- 1 apricot oat muffin
- 85g (250 mL) low-fat milk

Lunch:

- 400g (500 mL) red lentil soup,
- green salad, 15g. (15 mL) salad dressing with a light touch

Dinner:

- 1 serving pan chicken breast, 34 cup (175 mL) roasted sweet potatoes
- 1 egg omelet with vegetables

Day 23:

Breakfast:

- 28g dried steel-cut rolled oats
- 15g. peanut butter mixed with cooked oats
- Low Fat Milk

Lunch:

- Green Salad
- Grilled Chicken Breast
- ¼ cup Croutons

Dinner:

- Chicken & White Bean Stew
- 2 Whole Grain Bread

Day 24:

Breakfast:

- 2 bananas
- 2 apricots with dry fruits
- 43g (125 mL) skimmed milk

Lunch:

- 2 oz. (85 g) roast chicken
- 2 whole-grain bread pieces
- 28g. (10 mL) mayonnaise, mustard, lettuce, tomato if preferred
- 1 fruit

Dinner:

- 21g (175 mL) cooked couscous
- 1 dish white fish, green salad

Day 25:

Breakfast:

- 2 slices whole-grain or rye bread
- 1 poached or Sunnyside up egg
- 1 tiny avocado,

Lunch:

- 1 slice whole-grain bread, 28g. (10 mL) soft margarine
- 43g (125 mL) low-fat yoghurt
- Mexican baked eggs over black beans

Dinner:

- 85g cooked pasta (spaghetti, spirals, macaroni)
- 3-4oz (85-115 g) chicken, grilled or baked

Day 26:

Breakfast:

- 2 slices whole-grain or rye bread

- 1 boiled egg
- 1 apple, 1 banana

Lunch:

- Chicken salad with Tomatoes
- 43g (125 mL) low-fat yoghurt
- Green Smoothie

Dinner:

- Spinach Pilaf
- 3-4oz (85-115 g) chicken, grilled or baked

Day 27:

Breakfast:

- 2 slices whole-grain or rye bread
- 2 egg French Omelet
- 2 Peaches

Lunch:

- Over-roasted Salmon
- 2 Lettuce Wraps

Dinner:

- Roasted Lamb with sugar-free sauce
- 3-4oz (85-115 g) chicken, grilled or baked

Day 28:

Breakfast:

- 21g of toasted whole raisin bread and 1 slice of part-skim ricotta cheese
- 1 slice of fried Canadian bacon (one ounce)
- segments from half a cup of mango

Dinner:

- ounces baked cod
- 1 serving Grilled Ratatouille
- 43g cooked whole couscous
- 85g raw spinach tossed with 8.4g olive oil

Lunch:

- 2oz sliced turkey
- Mushroom Barley and Roasted Asparagus Salad
- 1 small whole pita bread
- 28.3g sugarless jam

- 85g fat-free milk

This diet plan when followed will form the ideal diabetic meal plan for you to follow.

DOWNLOAD YOUR GIFT NOW

The BONUS is 100% FREE

If, for any reason, you feel that there are cues for improvement or some errors, please kindly send me an email to the following address: **mrskellysmith719@gmail.com**. I will be very happy to welcome any criticism to improve the work and give more value to my clients.

On the other hand, if you liked the book, I would kindly ask you to post a review at this link, please copy and paste it on your browser if it doesn't work:

leave a review ~ diabetic cookbook

To download your bonus scan the QR code below:

Thank you so much, hope you enjoy your BONUS

Kelly

Manufactured by Amazon.ca
Acheson, AB